MESSAGES FROM BEYOND THE SUN

FRESH PERSPECTIVES FROM TODAY'S SPIRITUALLY INTELLIGENT LEADERS

ENGELHEIM PRESS, A DIVISION OF SHE{OLOGY} BY DR. ROBYN MCKAY

Copyright © 2024 by Engelheim Press, a division of She{ology} by Dr. Robyn McKay. All Rights Reserved. Apart from any fair dealing for the purposes of research or private study, or criticism or review, as permitted under the Copyright, Designs and Patents Act 1988, this publication may only be reproduced, stored or transmitted, in any form or by any means, with the prior permission in writing of the copyright owner, or in the case of the reprographic reproduction in accordance with the terms of licensees issued by the Copyright Licensing Agency. Enquiries concerning reproduction outside those terms should be sent to the publisher.

INTRODUCTION

Welcome to Engelheim Press and *Messages from Beyond the Sun*

A Note from Robyn McKay, PhD

Dear Reader,

This book is a celebration of fresh voices in the spiritual development space—intuitive channels, wayshowers, and spiritually intelligent leaders—who have forward to share their wisdom with the world. It is the culmination of a 6-month author development journey, guided by my new publishing division, Engelheim Press.

In Icelandic, "Engelheim" means *"Angel World"*; in Norwegian and German, it means *"Angel Home"*. In essence, Engelheim Press is *the home for the angels.*

This is the publishing house for gifted and talented leaders in the spiritual development space who *know* they're meant to write books that matter. It's a sanctuary for spiritually intelligent

INTRODUCTION

leaders who have reached a point in their lives where they can say, *"This is what I know right now,"* while honoring the truth that there is always more to learn.

What makes these authors especially unique is that, in addition to being spiritually and energetically adept, they are also highly educated and accomplished leaders in traditional fields such as psychology, engineering, business, finance, and the arts. They have been fearless in their willingness to share their intuitive insights and to act as bridges between the world of reason and that of intuition and spiritual knowingness.

Here at Engelheim, we hold a powerful intention: to publish the clearest and most refined spiritually-focused books on the market. I believe we can accomplish that because of our mission: to guide and develop the voices of spiritually intelligent leaders so they can confidently share their unique perspectives, deep wisdom, and innovative ideas that bring about healing and transformation.

There's a saying, "There's nothing new under the sun." One of the reasons that Engelheim Press exists is to challenge this age-old notion. Frankly, I don't believe it.

Together with our authors, we aspire to call forward and to create what's *beyond the sun*: new, fresh, and alive ideas, practices, and technologies.

Here at Engelheim, we create and we refine. We don't replicate.

Messages from Beyond the Sun represents the capstone experience of a 6-month author development journey, which I named "Write & Publish Your Channeled Text". During this program, each contributor committed to develop her voice, refine her intuitive channel, and write her "origin story" as well as share her "medi-

INTRODUCTION

cine" – her unique perspective that exists at the intersection between her professional expertise and her spiritual gifts. Through mentorship, community, and deep personal transformation, they've each emerged with stories and messages that illuminate the creativity and clarity they discovered along the way. But this book isn't just about who they've been. It's also about who they've become.

It seems to me that when you say what you truly think, when you channel the wisdom that arises from your highest calling, you become a beacon for those around you. You stand out, no longer echoing someone else's ideas, but instead as a singular, useful, and radiant voice of possibility.

The authors of *Messages from Beyond the Sun* have done exactly that. They've tapped into their channeled wisdom to write something that bridges the past with the future: something new, something alive, something I believe is profoundly needed for this time. Each chapter reflects their unique perspectives and medicine — gifts that create pathways for others to heal and to actualize.

These messages are channeled from the stream of consciousness that connects the authors with their original minds, the unlimited reservoir of creativity and innovation. Some of the messages are insightful and practical, others are whimsical, lively, and quite complex. To me, all are transformative and deeply meaningful.

Please remember, channeled messages are not meant to be Truth with a capital T. Rather, I think of channeled messages as fresh perspectives, a unique and useful way of seeing things. You're invited to receive what resonates for you and to leave the rest for another day, with love.

INTRODUCTION

But as you explore *Messages from Beyond the Sun*, consider that you're not just reading a book—you're experiencing the vibrancy of fresh perspectives and the potency of spiritual intelligence in action. These pages hold a collective mission: to inspire, uplift, and guide others toward their own creative, intuitive, and spiritual evolution.

As you read this book, consider it a touchstone—a living document of the human spirit's potential to create and to contribute. It's more than a collection of stories or advice; it's a beacon for those who seek to expand their own creative capacities, deepen their intuitive gifts, and answer their highest calling.

Thank you for joining us on this sunlit journey. May these messages illuminate your own path and inspire you to bring forward the wisdom, creativity and medicine that are uniquely yours.

In the end, this is what I know for sure: each of our authors are remembering how to write like the angels they are. To them and to all of us who are meant to write like the angels, welcome home.

All my best,

Robyn McKay, PhD

Founder, Engelheim Press, a division of She{ology} by Dr. Robyn McKay

CONTRIBUTING AUTHOR:

ALAINA PUFF, PHD

Dear Reader, a note from the author:

I have put forth deliberate thought as to why I decided to study psychology. I can recall my 17-year-old self sitting in my Psychology 101 lecture, during my freshman year of college, scribbling notes onto paper with such urgency, one could think they were going to vanish in thin air. Admittedly, I've always possessed a deep curiosity for understanding human behavior, particularly that related to child development. The manner in which we enter this world as fragile infants and seemingly miraculously develop into human beings. In pursuit of understanding how our environments can directly, or at times indirectly shape our perception of the world.

For much of my adult life, I've been committed to understanding how to best support children and their families in these ever-changing times we live in. And while my training was robust, it was also narrowly focused and didn't adequately consider the intricate nature of the human condition. By stepping outside the rigid lines of psychology in pursuit of my own healing, I was able to discover the medicine I share with you in this chapter. My life's purpose is to offer an alternative approach to better understanding the new generation of children that are coming onto this planet. Rather than pathologizing them with labels or focusing on their deficits, my intention is to deeply understand their unique strengths and gifts.

Although my intention for my mission has always been rooted in serving children and adolescents, I could have never anticipated the way my clients have deeply shaped me. When I reflect on my career, I'm confident those kids were divinely put into my path, as a means to provide that gentle nod from the universe that I was in fact on the right path.

In dedication of this chapter, I want to thank my mentors and all the families that entrusted me with loving and caring for their children. Thank you for stepping forward to embrace your children fully. I'm honored to continue this work.

1

ALAINA'S ORIGIN STORY

When I was training to become a psychologist, it was instilled in me the importance of adopting a 'blank slate' approach when working with clients. The therapeutic process can be viewed as a delicate, back-and-forth dance between you and your client. The therapist is present to merely hold space and guide the client through their respective journey. In many ways, I was trained to be a mirror for others, reflecting their light and darkness back onto them, so that they may find truth. Ironically, I did this long before I earned my credentials. I had been doing it my entire life – my words, presence, and beliefs were never truly mine but molded to what society deemed appropriate or expected for someone like me. It was through a gradual uncovering that I have arrived here to you today, fully exposed in truth of who I am and my purpose for this lifetime.

It is important to acknowledge my inherent discomfort with the process of writing to you. There is deep programming woven into the fabric of my cells, screaming at me to 'be quiet' or 'stay small' yet I refuse to listen. Only until recently, all the magic of my life happened behind a closed therapy office door when working directly with my clients. This is where I unknowingly began building a relationship with my intuition through my work with children and families. Perhaps that was intentional, to keep me hidden away from others; however, I now understand my mission and it is simply to share my words with you.

I've always had a keen interest in working with children. For me, youth represents hope in a world that often appears devoid of it. Children come into this world open and clear. They embody the playfulness and joy of human existence. As I traversed my way through the field of psychology, I possessed a deep understanding that I was meant to work with children, adolescents, and their families for these very reasons. From a point of practicality, I found children to be more flexible in their thinking and approach to the world, whereas adults tended to be hardened in their ways and thus more resistant to change. However, now reflecting on this undeniable pull, I realize that children possessed the magic of 'knowing' and my work was to help them retain it before the harsh reality of the modern world appeared to force them to forget.

In order to fully understand the process of becoming my authentic self, I need to take you back to the younger version of me. A little girl brought into the world, unplanned and surrounded by people who had no idea of my gifts and abilities. I came into this world five weeks early. I believe I was divinely guided to make my entry earthside because there was love and safety on the other side waiting for me. Despite the early stressors associated with an unplanned baby, my early childhood was marked by a time of innocence and love. I was showered in love by my parents, grandparents, and our extended family. I can recall that our home was often filled with laughter around the kitchen table, lights strung upon the Christmas tree, and a warmth that you could practically touch upon entering the threshold of our front door. I often wonder if my birth was a beacon of 'hope' in a long lineage of darkness that marked my family's narrative. Or perhaps it was a momentary distraction from the underlying turmoil that transcended through the family bloodline. Regardless of the cause, it was special and reflective of the complex nature of my childhood.

As a young child, I was extremely creative. Old family videos portray a joyful, jubilant, and carefree child who loved to sing and dance. Being an only child and the first baby in the family, much of my early years were spent in solitude, which I didn't mind. I can recall having many imaginary friends to keep me company. We would spend our time going on adventures to new worlds, solving problems, and simply being together in pure bliss. I can recall feeling deeply connected to nature, as I pulled weeds from the earth in the front yard and adorning them on my childhood dog like a crown. There was this walking trail near my grandmother's apartment that I would often beg my mother to accompany me on. Even though the overlook at the end of the trail gazed over a rundown trailer park, I referred to it as the "magic place" because through my eyes, it truly was magic. I was a very bright child, despite not having access to proper preschool or formal learning opportunities during my early years. I went on to attend kindergarten at the age of 4 years old, an entire year younger than my peers, and excelled in the class.

Not long after I was enrolled in school, I began experiencing symptoms that I now can connect to being a highly intuitive and sensitive child. I was painfully shy around my teacher and peers, despite being a boisterous child outside of the classroom. I developed stomach aches every day on the commute to school. I would come home exhausted, as my field would be clogged with not only my own energy, but those I had absorbed as I moved through the world. As I entered the third grade, I was unrecognizable to the child from a few years prior. My imagination had been siphoned by the need to survive my day to day life. Unfortunately, my parents were muddied in their own conflict and had no awareness that their daughter was "silently suffering" with every passing day. This is something, especially for young girls I often see in my work. Despite their ability to excel on paper, below the surface they are stripped of their sovereignty and living in a vigilant state of survival.

It all came to a head the summer before my 4th grade school year when my parents decided to separate and eventually divorce. With no notice, I was whisked out of my bed on a Saturday morning and moved across town to live with my mother. From this moment on, I knew my life would never look the same, as I burrowed deeper into myself. The once smiley and outgoing child was now merely a shell of myself. My system could not handle the enduring stress of my environment. I gained weight rapidly, my grades plummeted, and I struggled to make friends at school.

There is one distinct memory that comes to mind during this treacherous time. I was standing at the chalkboard in my fifth grade classroom along with a few of my peers. We were asked to diagram a sentence. My mind raced as I stared at the words glaring back at me. I could hear the soft scraping of the chalk against the board from my peers on either side of me completing their sentences. As if I had amnesia, I had no recollection of how to complete the task. I could feel my body fill with shame and embarrassment. Instead of crying out for help, I tucked my despair away and peered at my neighbors response as I scribbled on the board. This is how I survived elementary and middle school.

In my psychology training, I learned about disassociation, a defense mechanism where our brains intentionally disconnect from our surroundings in order to protect us from a perceived or real threat. This can result in a myriad of symptoms, with the most common being memory loss. Much later in graduate school, I would realize that disassociation had gotten me through the remainder of my childhood. I would find myself later in adulthood sitting on a therapist's couch sobbing at the absence of my childhood memories, wondering what happened to them and feeling incomplete. It has become clear that I was divinely held during that tumultuous time, my sensitive heart and kind soul could not bear the pain of the reality I was dealt, and it was simply tucked away in the depths of my mind in order to protect me. These gaps in my memory were part of my invisible armor that allowed me to move forward and eventually pull myself from that dark place, to return back to the light.

I went on to be a top performing student in my high school class, was a student-athlete, and held many leadership titles. Despite my longstanding poor performance on standardized assessments, I was able to get into my dream university that boasts an admittance rate of 11%. As a first-generation college student, I was a Division-1 student-athlete and double majored in psychology and education. I went onto graduate school where my success continued and eventually settled into my role as a school psychologist in public education. Although I would not describe myself as a naturally inquisitive learner, I found that the ivory walls of academia was a place where I could not only find success, but also a profound sense of safety and security. Unlike much of my childhood experiences, I was fully embraced in these academic spaces and celebrated for my contributions. All the external validation that was often missing from my early memories was now celebrated by my teachers and mentors. It was in the classroom that I can distinctly recall coming up for air for the first time since I was a young girl.

In my first role as a school psychologist, I was incredibly eager to apply my knowledge and expertise to help the students in my district. I was a quintessential go-getter. With every student I interacted with, I witnessed their limitless potential and joy, much like the younger version of myself. However, I was not adequately prepared for the stifling nature of public education. Growing up, it was instilled in me that education was a gateway to success in this world. It was a conduit for upward mobility and therefore something I should personally strive for. I carried this belief with me throughout my own education and training. However, being a public servant showed me the harsh reality of our education system. It is my observation that the true intention is to oppress children's gifts and abilities, much like it had done mine. Historically, the public education system was built on the premise of ensuring students could obtain jobs in factories and mills. That the measure of their 'worthiness' was reduced to job readiness skills. They would be equipped with the knowledge and skills to be deemed employable and a cog in the capitalist machine.

During this period of my life, I felt suffocated by my working conditions and similar to when I was a small child, I was given many signs by my body. I developed an auto-immune condition, gained 30 pounds seemingly overnight, and experienced intense 'brain fog' and fatigue. I found myself in the depths of burnout. Similar to the past, my intuition attempted to shield and redirect me from my reality. These 'warning signs' were presented to divert me from the path I was so stubbornly determined to keep walking. Unsure in how to proceed, I did what I knew best and returned to academia in pursuit of my doctoral degree, back to the place I knew guaranteed my safety.

I went on to successfully obtain a Ph.D. while steeped in some of the worst days of my life. On the surface, my pain was undetectable, yet the depths of me were completely depleted of light. My proverbial 'rock bottom' came at a bar on the evening following my graduation ceremony. Dressed in the traditional graduation garb, I sat in a booth surrounded by friends. I can recall staring into my drink feeling a deep emptiness inside of me. In that moment, I realized that a degree, accolade, or professional accomplishment would never quell the feeling that had remained dormant in me since I was a little girl: my desire to feel in alignment with the highest calling and truest form of myself. I felt alone in this world and completely devoid of any understanding of who I was. I had become unrecognizable to myself. This is the moment that changed everything, for this was the beginning of my spiritual awakening.

It was at this moment that I had grown exhausted running from what I had always known to be true. The essence of my soul, which had been locked inside of me up until that point. I simply could not sustain in this ongoing cycle of self-abandonment and denial of my truest self. Yet simultaneously I had no idea where to begin and can recall having thoughts like "am I crazy" for thinking this way. Despite not having a clear roadmap, in the coming months and years, I cracked myself wide open to reveal my highest timeline. A time marked by true surrendering to the divine. It was time to open myself back up to the magic of possibility and embrace the light within me. A time of remembering.

My spiritual awakening began by restoring the connection to my body. For most of my life, I existed in a dissociated state and was thus disconnected from my vessel. Through somatic practices, I began to experience sensations in my body. This was a profound experience for someone who spent the majority of their life living above the neck. My training in psychology capitalized on my tendency to over intellectualize, in that there was always a logical explanation for anything I encountered in life. However, I was no longer interested in logic or reason. As my connection to my body deepened, I began hearing whispers from my intuition. At first, it would be small gestures as I traversed daily life, and then it evolved into more profound messages coming through.

As I continued to intently restore the connection to my intuition, and ultimately with the divine, I was working in a private practice providing psychotherapy, while accruing my supervised hours for licensure. I had always been regarded as a talented and dynamic therapist, yet I never quite understood why since I didn't have robust training in this area. Unknowingly, when I found myself in a room with a client, I was able to clearly dial into their essence and use the messages that came through to guide our session. Meanwhile, I thought every therapist was doing something similar. I didn't realize at the time that this was my gift, this was my intuition speaking through me. As I continued down my own spiritual path, I began feeling the presence of intuitive messages coming through during my sessions with clients. I can recall moments where words would pass my lips that left me in complete astonishment, as I would hear such statements for the very first time. With this realization, I began honing my skills to be clearer than ever before in my sessions with clients by allowing these divine messages to seamlessly flow. In response, the children I was working with began cracking open in ways unlike before, sharing their experiences from past lives, memories from being in-utero, and elaborating on their psychic abilities. It was undeniable a major shift was occurring right before my eyes.

This brings me to the mission. While for much of my life I was a mirror to others and society, I now have a clear understanding of my life's purpose. By re-establishing a potent connection with my intuition, it is undeniable that I am here to serve as a steward for intuitive children. As the world continues to rapidly evolve, this new generation of children are coming onto the planet to heal it. We as a modern society have become over reliant on a mind driven by rationale and logic, yet this new generation of children possess unique gifts and abilities that challenge the status quo. These children are highly intuitive, making them extremely perceptive of their environments and present with a 'sixth sense' that enables them to tune into both the seen and unseen. I believe that they are here to restore the consciousness of this planet and it is our duty as parents and advocates to help them in doing so.

A key component of my mission is not only supporting intuitive children, but also their parents, which is ironic coming from someone who never wanted to work with adults. Given the vulnerable nature of children, their parents are responsible for the care, safety, and development of their gifts. I often share with my families that their child deliberately chose them to be their parents, and they must uncover as to why. The parents are a critical component of this mission because they provide the necessary nurturance to help children grow and evolve in their spiritual gifts. Without them, this process is elongated or worse, the children retreat into themselves indefinitely.

In my professional experience, when intuitive children fail to receive adequate nurturance in developing and honing their gifts, their systems become overstimulated and dysregulated. As a result, many children experience symptoms commonly associated with mental health disorders, such as anxiety, depression, and attention deficits and hyperactivity disorder. The symptoms are an expression of the underlying battle going on within these children. Similar to the one I experienced as a young child. Yet modern psychology fails to adopt this approach when treating pediatric mental health. For example, in my training many of the interventions were cognitively driven, with a focus on mental manipulation and reframing. While this is widely supported across the field of psychology, it does not integrate universal elements of the mind, body, and spirit. With the omission of a more holistic approach, my fear is that highly intuitive children are being inappropriately labeled with mental health diagnoses and thus pathologized, rather than uncovering and nurturing their spiritually intelligent gifts.

All this to say, I am here to challenge the typical thinking around how we support our young people, as it relates to their optimal development and well-being. I am here to guide the intuitive children and help their families better understand how to navigate this often complex, modern world. My training and expertise in psychology, enables me to understand the difference between spiritual intelligence and mental dysfunction, for it is often a fine line. Where I spent most of my life attempting to conform to the societal boxes laid out in front me, I can confidently say I have arrived home. The joyful little girl who still resides within me is filled with glee every time I work with one of these children. And the divine is gently guiding me, whispering wisdom into my bones, reminding me that I was and never will be alone.

2
―――

ALAINA'S MEDICINE

To see the world through the eyes of a child. A gift we cannot fully appreciate during our youth, yet we often long for as we age. Children possess an innocence and purity in a world that is often riddled in darkness, greed, and skepticism. They are shielded from the cutting edges of reality. It is the unadulterated hope and light reflected in a child's eyes that grounds you into the magnificence of the universe of infinite possibilities. We are all ushered into this world under this guise, a universal experience that unites humanity. However, unless it is intentionally nurtured, with time we begin to forget the magic woven into our cells and the unrefined desire to bring goodness to this world.

Based on what I know to be true, it is my purpose to instill and nurture this new generation of children. To protect them from an ever-evolving world designed to strip them of their gifts. To instill a sense of harmony and balance to the families they choose to join. Now more than ever, it is becoming evidently clear that the children coming onto this planet are uniquely equipped with intuitive and spiritually intelligent gifts to foster a profound sense of healing to anyone who crosses their path. However, modern society does not see it this way, in fact in many scientific circles today's children are pitied, as they are required to traverse the rapidly changing circumstances and are deemed more "at-risk" for negative outcomes than ever before. They are portrayed as helpless victims in a modern society of rapid consumption. Yet, I do not see it this way. I have witnessed firsthand how this generation of children possess the power to heal those who came before them. To assist the older generations in remembering what they always knew to be true about the world.

After working with hundreds of families, I have come to believe that children are some of the greatest sources of healing. They are brought into this world to reflect parts of ourselves that we are often resistant to uncover ourselves. For example, I have found in my work that for many parents, children expose their deepest wounds, which often developed during their own childhood. This often creates a concurrent experience of not only parenting our children, but re-parenting the younger version of ourselves. Moreover, the process of raising a child is multifaceted and rooted in a continuation of your own self-discovery as their parent. Children can be perceived as an invitation to deepen in your own healing journey and uncover your highest calling.

However, the modern mental health system does not maintain the same stance. Now more than ever before, we are observing the over-pathologization of children to better "explain" their behavior and symptomatology. Rather than viewing children as conduits for our own healing, there is this misperception that children are victims to our industrialized and ever-changing world. In my therapy practice, I witnessed children as young as

3-years-old come in for services with a litany of diagnostic labels attached to them. At such an early age, we are placing these children within prescribed boxes of what they are perceived to be capable of. One possible explanation is that parents, caregivers, and teachers are seeking possible 'explanations' to justify their own experiences with this new generation of children, which is a justified effort. However, by relying on a deficit-based perspective to best explain our children, we are stripping them of their gifts and utilizing medical interventions to quell their sense of wonder and imagination.

After years of working with children and families in the mental health system, I arrived at my own understanding of how to best support this new generation of children. I have come to believe that the mental health symptoms we are observing in children is not the manifestation of a true diagnostic condition, but rather the expression of an untapped gift, their intuition. When these children's gifts are not acknowledged or nurtured, they in turn will suppress them and hide them from the world. In doing so, this creates bodily dysregulation, where their nervous systems will be imbalanced compared to other children their age. Think about the feeling of holding your breath for as long as possible, towards the end it becomes completely unbearable. The same sensation takes place within these children. In turn, through continued suppression and existing under a dysregulated state, common 'symptoms' emerge, such as anxiety, depression, attention and behavioral challenges.

Reflective of the larger medical system, as psychologists we are trained to treat the presenting symptoms in our clients. And this is what I did for several years of my professional practice. Using evidenced-based strategies backed by scientific research, I poured myself into my clients and their families, with my focus always to alleviate their symptoms and produce positive outcomes. Despite all my efforts, I did not see the profound or even miraculous results I was hoping for and deep within myself, I knew we were putting a bandaid on a much deeper wound. Now I understand the root of this matter is that our children are coming onto this planet with gifts that require a new paradigm of parenting and education. That by nurturing these intuitive gifts, we are setting children up to thrive.

While many of us seek to obtain a sense of enlightenment and ascension throughout our adult years, I believe the children coming onto this planet today are propelled into this world at their highest point of ascension. That these living, breathing beings are the closest human form to the divine. For these children, there is no journey of unlearning deeply woven programming, healing past traumas, or reconnecting with their authentic self. They are coming earth-side as the most ascended versions of themselves, with gifts that are oftentimes unexplainable and perplexing to the adults who surround them. And with this, the responsibility falls on the parents and caregivers tasked to rear these children. The educators charged with teaching them and the communities built to protect and support them. We, as the adults, are here to nurture these young souls and ensure they remain connected to that ascension point. That the harshness of the world does not quell the magic in their soul.

After careful reflection, I was guided to share the stories of some of the incredible children I have worked with over the years who were undoubtedly intuitively gifted. By amplifying their voices, I aim to showcase their gifts in true divine perfection. May we continue to learn from them.

Case Study #1: Z

A shy 7-year-old girl entered my office with her mother on a Tuesday afternoon. She tucked her body carefully behind her mom as we shook hands and I ushered them over to the seating area. Z had large round glasses that seemed to encompass her entire face. She was polite despite her nerves. I watched as she scanned every inch of my office with her eyes. She jumped up when I suggested she check out my toy collection. She carefully examined each toy, as if she was taking inventory of them all. Her mother and I discussed that Z had been struggling with intense anxiety, causing her to have difficulty separating from mom and be successful at school. Z's mother added how this has caused immense disruption in the family's rhythm and parents were at a loss in how to support her. Z and her family had worked with a traditional therapist for over three years learning about anxiety and coping strategies to reduce symptoms. Yet, Z was still struggling.

My early work with Z was centered around building a safe and supportive relationship with her. She possessed a big heart that could practically burst out of her chest and with that came intense emotions. We spent our early sessions sprawled out on my office floor playing with dolls and talking about school. Z walked me through all the kids in her class, her perception of her soon-to-be retired teacher, and the subjects she enjoyed the most. As time progressed, Z would also come to share about the intense and at times debilitating stomach aches she would experience at school. The way she would sink down in her chair to make herself as small as possible, nearly invisible to everyone around her. Z was a good student, maintaining good grades and behavior at school, yet she was silently suffering day in and day out all while flying under the radar to every adult in the vicinity.

After understanding the severity of Z's experience, I met with parents to provide parent education on highly intuitive children. Z was not like many of the other children in her class. Her highly intuitive nature made her extremely perceptive to both the seen and unseen nature of her environments. For example, one day Z shared that the student next to her was having difficulty completing a math assignment. Z went on to describe in detail how she could physically feel the student's discomfort and the only way to alleviate it was to go over and assist him. Now while some may view this example as Z being empathic and helpful, it extends far beyond that. Z's ability to feel deeply was ultimately contributing to her dysregulation and subsequent anxiety symptoms. In addition, her taking on the role as "nurturer" and "caretaker" had already been deeply woven into her own perception of identity, by putting others before her own needs.

Upon speaking with her parents, I explained that it was insufficient to treat Z's anxiety alone because this was only an expression of the underlying root of it all, that Z was highly intuitive. We went on to nurture her intuitive qualities in future sessions. Exploring the mind and body connecting, regulating her nervous system using mindfulness and energy techniques, and with that her anxiety related symptoms began to decline. I taught Z about energy and how to protect her field in a manner that allows her to feel safe and comfortable. Throughout this work, I was also able to partner with Z's parents to uncover that they both were highly intuitive and observe them nurture their own gifts for the very first time as adults. It was an inter-generational container of healing, one I'll never forget.

Case Study #2: B

B entered my office like he owned the place. He had this palatable energy that was familiar, like coming home after a long stint away. As a short statured 10-year-old, B knew exactly why he was coming to therapy.

"Mom says I can't sit still" he spouted off to me when I asked my standard set of introductory questions. This proved to be absolutely true, as B was one of the most dysregulated children I had ever encountered. He was practically crawling in his skin as he moved about my office, closely examining everything. His mom appeared exhausted and at a complete loss on how to support her son. She shared that he was struggling in school and even with additional support B was getting removed from his classroom daily for distracting and disruptive behavior. At home, she described an ongoing power struggle between her and B. Altogether, she was exhausted and needed assistance.

In the coming weeks, B and I spent our sessions together playing board games and chatting about all kinds of interesting topics, such as airplanes, dinosaurs, and his annoying little sister. B was quite impulsive and would often act without thinking. One time, he accidentally knocked over a glass sand timer in my office, which he was quite fond of, and it shattered on the floor. B collapsed in a puddle of tears. "I'm sorry, Dr. Puff. I ruined everything and I understand if you don't want to see me anymore" he cried. I'll never forget this response because it shed light on everything I needed to know about B's internal state. I responded by comforting him and explaining that accidents happen and that this does not change anything between us. This interaction gave me a front row seat to how B's impulsive and dysregulated nature did a number on his self-esteem.

During one session, we were playing with Legos, when B turned to me and asked if he could share a story. I nodded and he proceeded to tell me about a memory from a time in his mother's womb. As the words passed through his lips with a concerted certainty, my eyes lifted to meet his. I found myself hanging on his every word trying to make sense of what I was hearing. He described his decision to arrive earth side early until his mother was in a car accident where she sustained a leg injury. B went on to share that he decided to wait until his mother was healed before making his great entry into the world. Admittedly, I was skeptical at first, attributing it to B's wild imagination or repeating a story he had heard from his parents. However, after the session I spoke with mom about the memory, and she was shocked as they had never mentioned the incident to him. We sat there sifting through possible explanations, but there were none. Developmental psychology tells us that children do not form concrete memories until about the age of three, yet this was not the case for B. I went on to learn so much from him.

As we progressed in our work together, B shared his experiences in the family's old home located in a historic neighborhood near downtown. He explained that he would often see and hear things that were not there, and this was an ongoing source of distress for him. Interestingly enough, B had not shared these experiences with anyone out of fear of being misunderstood or dismissed. As the whispered words passed his lips during one of our sessions about seeing a dark shadow in his room, I reflected on my training as a psychologist. The way we are programmed to stiffen our bodies when a client endorses common symptoms of psychosis. That a former version of myself would have immediately jumped to the line of thought that something is "wrong" with B given these experiences reflective of my training.

However, based on my current evaluation, B's clairvoyant and clairaudient gifts were developing quickly and likely contributing to his ongoing dysregulation and impulsivity. Through validation and education, I helped B develop a better understanding of his psychic gifts and how to utilize them. We practiced utilizing his power to cast out any negative energy stagnant in his old home and with that, things got better.

After making initial headway with B, I knew that I needed to loop his parents in on our work and lean on them for additional support to nurture his gifts. I brought both of his parents in for a family session where I explained the work I had been doing with B in our previous sessions and my suggested next steps. While B's mother seemed to be amenable to the words being thrown at her, I will never forget the look on his father's face. In retrospect, I now understand that B's father's ill reaction was because I was not only describing his son, but I was also describing a younger version of him. B's father had not taken a strong presence in our work together as a family, usually deferring to his wife. However, in our few conversations I was able to draw many parallels between B and his father. The difference was that B's father had deeply repressed his gifts from a young age and now as an adult was dependent on a slew of medications to feel much of anything.

Shortly after our family session, B's parents pulled him from therapy. His mom, apologetic on the phone, said they were going to trial medication and would reach out in a few months time. Unfortunately, I did not hear from them again. While this story continues to pull on my heart, it exemplifies the role us adults serve in helping our children reach their fullest potential. Without our support, the cycle will continue and in turn our children will suffer. There is no blame attributed to B's parents for pulling him from services. They simply were not ready to engage in the work of not only helping their son, but also uncovering parts of themselves, which I assert is one of the greatest challenges presented to us in this lifetime. My hope is that the several months I spent together with B, I was able to plant seeds of hope and wisdom. That he may know the gifts inside of him are real and spectacular - that he won't forget about them as he moves through the world.

ABOUT THE AUTHOR
ALAINA PUFF, PHD

Dr. Alaina Puff is the founder of Flow State Coaching and Consulting, a safe harbor for highly intuitive children, adults and families. She is a Nationally Certified School Psychologist turned Intuitive Coach. Dr. Puff offers an alternative approach to addressing common mental health "symptoms" when compared to the rest of modern psychology.

With her tagline 'the answers are already inside of you' Dr. Puff utilizes a mind, body, and spirit approach to holistically support her clients. She operates from a strengths-based perspective to assist her clients in deepening their relationship with their intuitive knowing to reveal their unique gifts and abilities. Dr. Puff is committed to helping children, adults, and families awaken their intuitive gifts, so that they can reach their highest callings.

Website: https://www.flowstateaz.com

Instagram: @dralainapuff

TikTok: @dr.alainapuff

CONTRIBUTING AUTHOR:

JACQUELINE CLARE PHILIP, MFA

Dear Reader, a note from the editor:

It's been said that what's most personal is also most universal - and I have to wonder what reader among us can't relate to Jackie's experience of being told over and over again that her art is too much, that she herself is too much. And yet, she preserves both in art and in life, and I believe that we are all made better for it.

Inherent in art, as I understand it, is the artist's invitation to feel *something, for the artist to invoke a reaction in her audience.*

In Part 1, Jackie's lyrical prose transports her readers back to her childhood, to a time when her inner world was alive with connection, her imagination vivid. We see a stark contrast to the others in her world who simply could not see and did not understand her inner world, her intuition.

Some artists achieve this through the use of dark, even shocking, provocation, a series of edgy, aggressive jabs at the audience's consciousness. Jackie, on the other hand accomplishes the felt experience through her loving honesty and her ability to channel light and the precision with which she calibrates and places every color, every hue on her canvas.

Throughout the chapter, she writes in the third person, providing us with a re-telling of her childhood from a higher perspective, what I think of as her most-realized self or her channel.

From the vantage point of her channel, Jackie shares her experience of feeling ostracized, bullied, and misunderstood first in her childhood and later, as the vibrancy and luminosity of her art emerges, by the art community. If her critics' reactions are any indication, I strongly suspect that they did indeed, feel quite a lot from her vibrant paintings - just not what they were comfortable with or familiar with the feelings Jackie's work invoked in them. Rather than explore it, they rejected it. Let us not make the same mistake.

In part 2, my favorite part about part 2 is that Jackie once again writes in the third person, a channeled flowing message from her *channel*. As readers, we are invited along to explore and discover the nature and essence of her medicine, her gifts. We learn how she herself has come to understand her masterful use of color and light to create canvases filled with both that activate and evoke higher emotions of love, joy, peace, and wellbeing.

3

JACQUELINE'S ORIGIN STORY

CHILDHOOD

As a very small child illuminated under the sun, brought up under the sun, held by the sun, you're sitting under a tree in the dappled light of the mid afternoon heat, talking to the tropical pink flowers, the hummingbirds, the trees, the tree frogs, the dragonflies.

You are feeling their energy.

You are hearing them.

You are them.

You are part of their world.

I invite you to join me on a journey, a visual journey, a journey of discovery, a traveller's tale of bees and majestic trees, of sunlit seas and blue, blue skies, a journey of hue and of light, of becoming the artist, the innervator, the channel, the visionary.

You are stardust, starlight.

You can telepathically tune in and hear what the birds and animals and insects say to you.

You connect with them and they connect with you.

You are one with them, no separation.

But then your mother is calling you. " Where are you? Stop hiding, come out. What are you doing?"

You tell her "I'm talking to the animals, the trees, the grass, the insects. I love them. They're my friends"

"Don't be silly. Stop talking nonsense. Come, come."

"But I was," I protest, " I was talking with them. I was talking with them and the fairies. Look, look at my wings. I'm a fairy too."

"Don't talk nonsense. Be quiet. That's not true"

My mother admonishes me further.

"Don't be silly. Stop talking nonsense. Come, come."

And you were so hurt, stunned. You couldn't believe it. Who else were you to talk to? Your little brother couldn't speak. You loved going near and talking with them, the plants, the animals.

But then you were told to stop being silly.

You decided that it was better, safer, to say nothing in case you were admonished, misunderstood, not loved.

Didn't fit in.

And when you went to school, you would stand and watch and observe.

Observe what's going on, but felt too frightened to say anything in case they said you were silly or stupid. You didn't know what you were to say.

You didn't know how to communicate with the other children.

And you kept quiet.

You felt that something was wrong.

This is what's around us.

How can you not see?

How can you not hear?

How can this be?

You remember standing in line at school and not really knowing what to do or say.

And you felt very sad.

You felt different, you felt ostracized, cast off.

So you stopped thinking about it, stopped talking about it, tried to fit in. But you knew that difference was always there.

Not exactly talking in your head, just a presence.

A presence, a presence all around.

Like wings touching you, fluttering by.

It was comforting, but scary at the same time. And when you got older, you just remained very quiet. Became more introverted.

You were bullied.

You felt ashamed, but you didn't know what the shame was about.

Shame that you were different.

Shame that you didn't fit in, even though you were very bright, fast, the teachers didn't think you were because you were very quiet, not noticed.

Becoming the Artist

It was only later in the last years of school when you were in the art room, where you could find solace, being alone.

And you knew that there was something special happening.

That you could draw, you could paint.

It was fascinating.

It was a relief.

A relief to find that connection, to find that connection to a creative source.

And at art school, you flourished, you excelled, painted bigger and brighter than everyone else.

You were told to tone it down.

Why? It was the luminosity they didn't like.

The frequency of the luminosity.

It was too big for them to handle, too extreme.

The frequencies were different.

And you didn't tone them down.

Instead your paintings got bigger and bolder because you were bored painting small and dark.

It was in the hues, the layers of hue.

And when you painted in the landscape you felt connected and the landscape emerged through you. You were part of the landscape, part of the land, the vines, the trees, the earth, the sky.

And the paintings came through you, through your eyes, through your hands.

They flowed, they flowed.

They were channelled paintings, acknowledged.

Location: Bali, Indonesia

And then when you were in Bali, that's when you became more aware and connected again.

Vitalised to the ritual of painting, the ceremony of painting, the ritual all around, the connection to the rice paddies, the multiple hues of that extreme emerald green, the sound of the insects, the sky above. Alone in the paddy fields, it was exhilarating, expansive.

True connection, infusing those vibrant, luminous frequencies of hue.

It was a turning point. It was a turning point for you. It was a deep, deep, deep connection, an elemental connection.

And you knew then, that you had to change how you were painting.

You had to change the process to build the layers of luminosity, layer by layer, layer by layer.

Capturing the light, infusing the light, weaving light into the paintings.

They became richer and richer, more and more luminous.

A rich tapestry of light and hue.

Simplicity of composition, purity of hue, pure raw pigment, pure vibration, pure light essence.

It felt so good, it felt so expansive.

Location: United Kingdom

And when you returned to the UK, you were told, your paintings are too bright, they are too luminous, they're too much.

Too much, too much, tone it down.

You felt that you had to hide your light, hide your essence to fit in.

The artists didn't like it, the galleries didn't like it, because they could see, but not understand, the difference in what you've created.

They felt their strength, their intensity of hue.

It was a time when things felt heavy and dark, and alone.

Ostracized for being creative, for being more and more luminous.

Again, it was hidden, dimmed, dimmed, dimmed right down.

Turning the light right down, searching for connection. Always feeling that there was something missing. You had the inner strength, but not the inner knowing.

What were you to do, but stay hidden. Almost running away, moving to a different country, moving to the other side of the world.

Where again, you awakened to that connection, to the sea, the sky, the land.

Breathing in its expansiveness, infusing it and again, it trickled back into your paintings.

A rich tapestry of light and hue.

A richness, a jewel-like richness.

The capacity to hold more light.

But it was pushing energy, pushing energy to try harder, be harder, be self-critical, be harder on yourself.

Prove yourself, be stoically independent.

To be, and do, and do, and do, and do, and do, and do.

Hard work, hard struggle.

But always creating something new, always on the edge of creating something unique.

Always searching for that missing piece, that missing connection.

Finding solace in the paintings, but not in others.

Feeling that isolation.

Being the one that was so different.

Feeling so different, so unseen.

Travel and location, location and travel.

The physical aspect of moving around this earth. This has been a significant aspect of your life, your journey.

Sipping and receiving nectar from place to place.

Each place holds its own frequency, its own hue, its own light, its own expression.

"I'd like to share with you a deeper layer, a deeper unfolding to three locations in particular. Barbados, where I grew up, Bali and New Zealand. In each place, experiencing a deeper anchoring and sense of homecoming"

Location: Barbados

Your life in Barbados, as a child from under the sun, under the light beams, you could communicate telepathically with the trees, the birds, the grasshoppers, the flowers, and the water.

Yes, you talked to the sea.

You talked to the water, the sea enraptured you.

The sea was your delight.

The sea was calling you.

The light on the sea was calling you, speaking to you.

The light beams, the sparkles were your language.

The hues of the light were your language, playing on the beach, sitting on the beach, watching the sea.

Even as a very young child, you connected deeply with the sea.

It was the light on the sea, the light sparkles, that hue, that iridescent aquamarine.

This was your elemental playground.

This was your jewel, your playground that you absorbed, that you connected with, connected to.

This was your sensory playground, your light language playground.

It was your joy, your de-light, and you didn't understand why others didn't see it.

You'd say, "look, look, look, look at the fairies of light on the sea.

Look at the sparkles, look at the colour".

You loved that hue, you connected with that hue.

It's always been with you.

It's the hue of your eyes, drinking in the hue of the sea.

It was your delight, it is your delight, it is part of you.

Because you are the keeper of the original waters, the infinite waters, drinking it in, drinking in the hues, drinking in the light, anointing others with it, anointing the access point for the original mind and the palms of the hands.

You spoke in light language.

You are the keeper of the cosmic waters, the guardian, the anointer.

This is your gift, your medicine for others to experience.

The light, this amazing blue light, encompassing the blue of the sky and the blue of the water.

Blue topaz, lapis lazuli, aquamarine, ultramarine from across the seas.

The yellow golden light, the golden sunbeams.

These come through you and into your paintings.

You alchemise them into your paintings.

This is your gift, your gift for hue-manity.

You are a conduit for those hues, the water, the light, the sky, blended through you, infused through you, spiralling through you, weaving a web of light and hue.

Location: Bali

And Bali was a connection point too, a connection point to original frequencies, a frequency that you experienced in the land, on the land, in the sky, the fields. Being in the paddy fields brought you into alignment, to connect, to connect deeply.

What you could see, what you express through your hands, through the paintbrush, through the visceral feeling of being in that environment, the expansiveness, the hues, the breeze, the insects, the ducks, the way the paddy fields blew in the wind, the light, the sound, the humming sound, the sound was singing to you, the light was pouring into you, you felt as if you were within another time and space.

An experience of being above the landscape, being in the landscape, of flying around the landscape, your wings were attached, ignited.

Your hands send energy into the paintings, your eyes absorb, optimise and activate you and everything around you, a Oneness.

A time to be alone and for us to be there with you, to sit beside you, to be you.

You allowed your channel into your vessel, your container, it was with great joy we came and it was with great joy you received.

The messages that we sent, the light frequencies, the light language, the sounds, the breeze, the sounds of the insects, the sound of the ducks, this was you coming into your highest point of ascension, this is your pivotal turning point, your re-membering, your awareness of more than you and a paintbrush.

Of being ensconced in the life of ritual and beauty as are the Balinese, life and death, life and beauty, expressing, expressing through their hands, the dance of the long nails, expressing their divinity, through their hands, to optimise the frequency.

This is what you do, this is what you know you do, through your hands, through your eyes, through your smile, through your presence.

This essence, this knowledge, you kept it, you nurtured it, you felt it, but at times you forgot it, at times you became disconnected.

Disconnected.

Location: New Zealand

But then the frequencies in New Zealand brought you back to that real connection point, that spaciousness, that expansion, that time to be alone with your paintings, to be alone by the sea, to experience the changing light, the hues of the water.

The skyline, the hill line, you saw it all, you observed it, you watched it, you became it, that is what you are expressing, the essence of what you are alchemising, the essence of the hues, the light, the sounds, the weather, the birds, all of it, you are pouring it into your paintings, the vessel for your paintings.

Those times, a time of expansion, a time to reconnect, a time to experience and connect with us, connecting with us through your eyes.

The vastness of it all.

And those experiences of deep hurt, deep pain, physical pain, were to bring you back into your body, to bring you into the light but also to hide your light for you to feel safe, as you did not feel safe to be all of who you were.

It was time for you to go inward, you were ready but the earth was not ready for you.

The ways of being were not ready for you, it was not ready to be expressed, shared, there was too much separation.

You were brought to your knees and this experience gave you strength, the strength to look from within.

The strength to experience harmonising energies, the healing frequencies, through the physical touch of massage, qigong, of acupuncture, for you to feel the energy, the life force qi flow through your body, reawaken to become whole and know that this energy flows from within, the energy of light, the energies to restore, to heal, to come together as a pure energetic vessel, to be ready as an energetic vessel when the time was right.

You are sharing this experience, this wondrous journey, this healing journey, this uplifting journey and how you became a channel, an innervator, a messenger.

You have experienced great highs and great lows.

You came to know that you are your body, not just your mind, and that this wisdom resides in your wholeness.

The purpose of your healing journey was for you to know your body, to know your essence, to know your true self, to know that you are whole, you always were whole.

Now you can share for others to feel this innervating aspect which you've experienced throughout your life, of looking inside of you for the way forward, to create a pure vessel for your channel, for you to re-member, to re-member your gifts, your life now as the intuitive channel to be in flow, to innervate, illuminate and bring the harmonising energies of serenity and joy to Hue-manity.

*Hue = original colour

4

JACQUELINE'S MEDICINE

Your day begins as a celebration of life, your special time, of being in nature, of nature, communing with the trees, your special lime tree, grounded on the earth and held by the sky, infused by the sunlight, moving the body, connecting with your body, your morning engagement with qigong and be-ing with your intuitive channel.

All of this you bring to the studio, a reverence for the paintings, to the painting, to the palette, the pigments, the paint, the canvas, beautifully prepared with soft chalky gesso, the surface to receive the hues and light, the stroke of the brush, the texture of the canvas, the aroma of pigment and oil.

An intentional engagement, a daily conveyance allowing the paintings to come to life, through you.

A vital dance of paint, a substance of energetic liquid hue, a consciousness, mixing, painting, scumbling and brush marks, weaving a web of light intelligence around the canvas, radiating, permeating, infusing, layer by layer, hue by hue, every nuance, every mark, every brushstroke, a celebration, a celebration of life giving breathing, communicating hue.

Of hue and light and paint, in-spired, in-spirit, in-breath, breathing it into life, breathing it into light, bringing it into physical form.

Creating a physical vessel, a physical container from which to sip this joyful nectar.

This potent elixir flows through your body, through your eyes, through your hands, into the artwork, in a flow that only you can make sense of.

Only you know how to interpret, only you know how to mix these sensations of hue.

This is what makes your paintings unique.

It is your wisdom and your knowledge which activates and synthesises these sensations of hue into your signature artwork.

It is your wisdom and experience that is being brought to the fore to be expressed for others, for hue-manity. It is your experience and your energetic essence and the way that you can see and hear and feel everything around you all at once.

You are able to do this without becoming overwhelmed.

You are able to do this because you have accepted to do this and you have, in a way, normalised what others can not do.

To be present and to be aware of all these sensations around you at all times. It is in your recognition and the unique abilities that you have acquired from all your experiences, to create this important work, to offer this great gift.

It is for *hue-mans* to receive from your experience, all the experiences, the wholeness, the journeys, the wanderlust, the travels, physical journeying and shape shifting.

You are being infused all at once into your paintings, nuances, nuances of hue, nuances of light, nuances of meaning, nuances of the relationship between you and your eyes and your hands and the paint and the paintbrush, the way you respond to the sensations of hue.

These are unique to you.

To a certain extent, these skills have been learnt through practice, study and diligence but also your great capacity for curiosity, curiosity for everything in the world, curiosity for how paint works, how hue works, you being in the world, absorbing this light language, this language of hue, the original colour codex.

This is what you are bringing to the forefront.

Your experience of hue and light, this energetic substance, this sensation of hue, the way they resonate, the way they communicate, interact, and your role as a mentor, a tutor, gives you the capacity to show, express and share your knowledge and your wisdom, your experience as a master artist who can orchestrate, mix and calibrate, who can know the tiniest minutiae of hue and how it works and how it interacts, to channel these frequencies and codes, these frequencies of consciousness and light.

It is in the sentient of the hue that you are channeling these frequencies and codes, this light language, to be received through the eyes and into the physical form.

Through the harmony and balance of your hues, through the harmony and balance of the physical form, it is the same frequency. It is the frequency of your hues that are innervating for hue-mans, so that they too can feel that calmness, that balance, that coherence.

To feel that relief, that nutritive experience, to feel the possibilities, to feel the integrity of who they are and their connection to the earth, to nature, you are showing them that connection and the disconnection, to re-connect them to their inner light, their inner wisdom to bring them home to their body, through a tangible connection in physical form.

And when you look at the sea and when you look at the lake, you see the water, you are absorbing that harmonising frequency, that harmonising hue, that harmonising light.

That frequency is the potency, the medicine for the hue-mans and the earth.

The natural system requires nutrients from the sky and the water, to optimise the liquid in the body and the earth. Frequencies of coherence and harmonic alignment.

For the planet, for *hue-manity*, for each individual.

You are the guardian of the original waters, the aqua, the aquamarine, the blue topaz, the original hue, which is reflected from above and below.

Because the sky is water, and water is the sky, it is one.

There is no separation.

You are bringing in the codes that allow hue-mans to feel serenity, to bring them into resonance, coherence, a calmness which can bring great relief, a feeling that many *hue-mans* are not able to feel.

This is the joy that you're bringing into the world, you're bringing in the joy of the hues, the joy of the sensations, the joy of the light.

And when *hue-mans* see your paintings and breathe them in and smell them and connect with them and feel them, it by passes the mind and brings it in to their physical form.

Hydration, like plants secreting nectar, the nectar and juice that has flowed into your being, into your paintings for *hue-mans* to experience.

You are pollinating from your experiences and bringing in the original interaction of hue, nourishment for the body, fluidity and flow for the body, fortifying the physical form.

You are a wonderful artist, a creatrix of light and hue, a creatrix of essence of light and original hue, infusing your life, your world, the world, your paintings with light and hue.

Frequencies of wholeness, of love and light, of illumination, illuminating others, illuminating their physical form, illuminating their consciousness, illuminating the cells within their living bodies with fluidity, pure cosmic water, pristine, pure essence of water, expanding the light and water, expanding the frequency, full - filling their body, full - filling them, so that they can expand and shine their light.

So that *hue-mans* can feel expansive, satiated.

You and your paintings are activators, activations and sensations infused with hue and light to bring the body into harmonic resonance, into balance, to innervate the liquid waters in the living body, to activate the liquid waters of the earth.

We are water.

And this is a water planet.

Anointing others with soul liquid, to innervate the fluid in the body, hydration for the body.

Drinking it into your organs, your eyes, your bones, a deep cleansing, a waterfall of nourishment, liquid hue filled light, moving through you, anointing you.

And when this is brought into resonance, it expands and fills with more frequency, more light, more energy. It brings the body out of stress.

It brings the physical form into harmonic resonance, into serenity. It surrenders and lets go. It surrenders and lets go of the stress, the aches and pains, the tensions, emotional release, physical release. A sigh of release.

The waters of the body, the crystalline waters of the body are magnetic. And the more that this liquid is activated in your *hue-man* form, the more magnetic you become.

An effervescence of energy, an effervescence of light, an effervescence of joy, love.

Abundance flows to you, flows through you.

An infinite flow of abundance.

Your paintings are a conveyance of energy, a switch, you're switching on the serenity button, the calm.

To be more full - filled, to be filled, filled, filled

Filled with light, filled with frequency, filled with hues, to live in abundance and joy.

You are an activator of the original colour codex.

You are re-membering the original colours.

Pure hue, you feel them and how they resonate.

They speak to you.

You create them in perfect harmony, you restore them to original frequencies, original frequencies of light.

Light spectrum of light-sourced hue, imbued, infused and mixed with light to expand their capacity to hold more light.

To hold more currency.

You are returning them to their true nature, their true essence.

Their life-giving properties.

They are sources of light refraction.

Pure colour, pure essence, pure light.

Your paintings are a gift to bring to earth, the frequencies of love, frequencies of joy, imbued with beautiful blues and golds and yellows and oranges, high vibrations that fill the body, expand the body, expand the body to receive more, to receive more and give more, to feel more spaciousness, expansion. An innervation to allow you to receive, an innervation of expansion, expansion of wondrous frequencies from the sky, the sea, the waters, the flowers, the trees, the earth.

Through your paintings you are bringing in these conveyances of de-light, illuminating light, illuminating the water in the cells, sparking them with light, sparks of energy, frequencies of light, each cell of water being lit up, expanded to receive more light, to receive more energy, to receive the sun, to receive the hues, to receive and allow the waters in your cells to expand.

To expand and fill you, to full - fill you, full - fill you with sparkling water, sparkling light lit water, creating an effervescence of energy and joy in your body, an effervescence of sparkles of light, shimmering light, to create a flow of light and fill the water and the *hue-man* form with light.

This is the stream of consciousness that you communicate through your paintings as a connection for *hue-mans*, a heart-to-heart communication, a magnetic communication, expanding the water in the cells is magnetic, a magnifying of light, of joy, of love in the body, for the body, for the vessel, so that the vessel can function fully, optimally.

And when others engage with your paintings, it can bring them into harmonic alignment, calm, a flow of serenity and little by little expand, expanding this frequency day by day, a daily interaction of expansion, of harmony and balance, serenity and joy.

Your artwork is infused and alchemised through your eyes into your physical form, through your senses, through your emotions into your vessel. And when hue-mans see your paintings, there is an immediate recognition, a soul to soul connection, and the living body can be fully sourced, nurtured, and re - member, what it feels like to be in divine perfection.

This is your gift to *hue-manity*.

To bring calm, peace and serenity.

Joy and love through your paintings.

Your paintings bring frequencies of relief, of calm, of light. This abundant, glorious light that you see all around you, captured in paint, infuses through you, melding your light with the light of the painting.

A conduit of beautiful, shimmering light.

Others see it through their eyes, they drink it in and the light filters through their physical form.

Hue-mans can feel stress, pain in their body permanently.

This is what you experienced. You have that knowledge, that knowing to be the change for *hue-manity*.

Their eyes see it, their bodies feel it, by passing the mind. They feel the energy, the powerful energy, sensate through the paintings into their physical form.

This will enlighten, enlighten, illuminate. The light will be filled and illuminated in their physical form. Illumination.

You are the giver of illumination.

Illumination.

You are the giver of light.

Infused with the original colour codex.

Each hue has its own potency, each nuance has its own potency.

Each paint mark has its own potency.

Each brush stroke has its own potency.

It is all infused through the layers.

Layers of light, layers of frequency, layers of light language.

Infused, sometimes hidden in plain sight. Sometimes there and sometimes not there, but they are there.

You are bringing all of your senses into your paintings.

Your sight, your hearing, your smell, the touch, the being in the landscape.

Shapeshifting into what you are painting and you become the painting.

The essence of what you see.

The essence of nature.

The essence of the universe.

The essence of light.

The essence of sunbeams.

You bring it all into your light being, to reflect back to others, what you have seen and witnessed and absorbed.

By be-ing you, by be-ing your painting.

All is one.

You are the painting, you become the painting.

And even when you are not painting, it is in your presence.

It is in your eyes, your hands, your smile.

When you see others, you see them.

You see them fully.

You see their soul.

There is a soul to soul connection.

In the same way that your paintings are a soul to soul communication.

You are offering this gift, this medicine.

Exquisite paintings that radiate beauty, a threshold, an invitation to step through a portal of *hue consciousness*.

A doorway, a portal to their own signature frequency.

Each painting conveys a message, a channelled message, a message for each individual.

An interactive experience, a painting, a container which others can relate to and connect with everyday, as it radiates and hums in their home, illuminating their space with frequencies of consciousness.

A ripple effect for all those who pass by your paintings.

They are all innervated by it, enraptured.

They are a beautiful part of the tapestry.

The weaving of light.

The weaving of light frequencies reflected onto others.

They are miraculous.

Frequencies that activate the body's natural power and luminous nature.

This is the sum of your experiences, the truth of what you know, this gift that you are offering to the world.

To acknowledge and share what you have always known, to have travelled this journey for others, with others, for you to re-member, knowing that this is your soul's mission, knowing that this is, what you came here to be, to share, and to activate millions, to activate this pure light, this pure hue, the original waters into their be-ing, into the earth, for hue-manity.

This is the call.

This is your role as the artist, the channel, the anointer, the innervator, the messenger, the visionary, to share this wisdom and knowledge of the original colour codex and the original waters with luminous, lustrous, hue.

It is miraculous.

It is a miracle in the making.

Your paintings are a blessing, they radiate love and light.

They radiate sunshine.

You are absorbing the sunshine into the paintings, activating, the crystal clear waters, the shimmering light, the divine essence.

To innervate the planet, to uplift *hue-manity*, to uplift consciousness, the intelligence of the vessel, pure illumination, expanding around the earth, lighting up around the earth, pure light, pure essence, pure light being, weaving a web of light.

Healing *Hue-manity*, one painting at a time.

ABOUT THE AUTHOR
JACQUELINE CLARE PHILIP, MFA

Since completing her postgraduate studies with an MA in Fine Art, from The Royal Academy, Schools, London, Jacqueline Philip is the recipient of many prestigious awards and scholarships and has lectured in Art Schools in London, Florence and Auckland.

She has exhibited widely with solo exhibitions nationally and internationally and her paintings can be found in corporate and private collections in the UK, Europe, H.K, Australia and New Zealand, the Caribbean and USA.

Jacqueline creates a unique harmonic resonance through her channeled paintings and writing, by weaving a rich tapestry of luminosity, words and hue, in service to her mission, to "Heal Hue-manity one painting at a time".

www.jackiephilip.com

CONTRIBUTING AUTHOR:

JUDY EGGLESTON, M.ACC

Dear Reader, a note from the editor:

Judy grew up on a farm in the middle of America, in the middle of the last century.

She writes, "Nature sparked my curiosity as a child, and I was fortunate to be able to explore and play in it starting at a very early age. Children's books with stories of fantasy and folklore engaged my intellectual curiosity. But playing and engaging in nature nurtured my lifelong curiosity to learn about things I did not understand and could not read in a book."

In Judy's origin story, she brings forward snapshots from her childhood including conversations with nature, her love of flying, and early experiences that shaped her relationships and understanding of nature and her role in the world. She's taken this approach so that in her second chapter, you, the reader, may understand that her intuitive intelligence and lifelong connection with nature are what enable her to work with energy in ways that are both highly useful and singular to her experiences.

5

JUDY'S ORIGIN STORY

DISCOVERY IN NATURE

THE BUTTERFLY, THE TREE, AND ME

The cool crisp air flowed gently over the top and through the tent.

I was in heaven, camped out in our farm's backyard, a state of bliss for me, as a seven-year-old farm girl.

A monarch butterfly flew in and landed on my pillow for a morning chat about the day ahead.

My guide for the day, she led me through the grass and trees, in a wondrous state of joy and curiosity. Following a thing of beauty, she had an elegant grace, as she flew in front of me, chatting about her surroundings. Soon, I sat and leaned against the bark of an elm tree and my butterfly landed on my leg. We talked about her life and what it was like to be a butterfly. I felt the tree chuckle in agreement, and he joined us. His long life, I discovered, was full of history. He shared how he began, as the wind carried his winged seed and this was where he had landed. Soon came rain, which helped him connect to the earth. The moisture provided the perfect bed for him to begin growing, which was where we were sitting now.

Little did I know at the time, but later in life I would become a pilot and let my own winged adventures enrich my life. That morning, it was just a tree, the butterfly and me, laughing about our good fortune to live in the simple diversity of nature, a freedom not everyone gets to enjoy.

Later that morning, the butterfly and I joined a bouquet of prairie flowers in a tall grassy area. The flowers eagerly engaged us, chatting about their individual hues to attract certain insects to join them. For me, listening to their collective whispers was like hearing a choir of voices in the flower patch. Apparently taking turns talking was not so much a thing. Here on the prairie, I learned to be a conductor. Harmonizing the flowers into a symphony by focusing on one of them at a time. The different flowers formed a colorful painting in the morning air. Bees and other flying things I could not name joined them, and this thought came to me: the flower patch was a buzz, and they all loved the company.

A few years later in school, I was to learn about pollination and how they worked together. For now, I just enjoyed the simple beauty and the walk with my new butterfly friend. I decided to name her Princess; she was my royalty for the morning. Suddenly, a voice rang through the air and I was being called to eat lunch. I said goodbye to the Princess and turned back for the house.

The Turtle's Wisdom

Another warm, bright afternoon I went to the river to play in the cool flowing water and sat on the bank next to a turtle. The turtle talked about his life in the river and the territory he never strayed far from. This is where I learned not to take a turtle to the backyard from the river. And why the next morning when I looked for my friend in my backyard, all I could see were the turtle tracks that led back to the river. I named the turtle Frank, but his nickname was The Wise One.

Frank talked about turtles having a territory, a part of mother earth. I've found that they, in many ways, are the wisdom keepers of the land and water. Most afternoons I spent in the river, he remembered me and would come check and listen to my stories, just as I listened to his stories. The lesson I learned from Frank, The Wise One is to remember to listen when traveling to new parts of the earth. To listen to the local wisdom and to share my own experiences, a practice which enriches everyone's lives. To this day I have a brass turtle sitting on my desk. It's my favorite paper weight and more importantly as a reminder of the wise conversations I had with Frank, on the riverbank as a child.

The Bees

Walking back to the farmyard, I took a shortcut through a luscious green alfalfa field with the small purple flowers flowing in the breeze. On this day, the field was buzzing with hundreds of honeybees. The thought of busy bees brought a grin to my face. As I sat at the edge of the field, two bees quickly flew past me to enjoy the alfalfa clover. In the tops of the alfalfa, the bee's wings constantly flapped up and down, as they hovered, almost stationary. It puzzled me why we have wise owls, when it's the bees who hold so much wisdom and consciousness. It was much later in life I would understand the importance of bees, for now as a girl, I simply enjoyed the buzzing sound of the bees and watching them dance with the flowers in the alfalfa field.

My Intrigue with Water

My intrigue with water, other than drinking water or taking baths, began when I was a small child, just three years old. I remember taking my clothes off so I wouldn't get them dirty... I think... and then promptly sitting down in a mud puddle in the farmyard, where I discovered the joy and exploration of splashing in the water. Looking back, this moment was the beginning of my lifelong relationship with water. It wasn't until much later that the water itself and the beings living in it interested me.

But the river water, how it flows with ease, occasionally interrupted by a beaver dam and having to reroute itself through the sand in another direction always drew me in. Throughout my childhood, I regularly swam in irrigation ditches, as well as in lakes and ponds on my family's river land. In my later years, I experienced freedom, curiosity and great enjoyment on the water, water skiing, sailing, windsurfing, open water swimming, and paddle boarding.

The Birds: Peacocks, Blue Jays, and Robins

One of my 4-H projects was raising peacocks, which added to my fascination with flying things. The peacock's wake-up calls in the morning sounded more like someone yelling for help than the traditional alarm clock. It didn't take long to realize the importance of telling new house guests that we were all okay if they heard the peacocks in the morning.

This one afternoon, my peacock greeted me with fanned tail feathers, welcoming me back home after I'd been away for a while. He led me to the backyard and showed me a new patch of grass, his place for us to have a conversation and pretend we were having tea. The conversation was a full update of what happened at the farm while I'd been gone. A blue jay came by and noisily talked about a lunch of fresh corn kernels dropped on the ground. We adjourned our tea, and the two of them went to peck away the corn kernels.

Next, I walked over to my sand pile beneath my grandmother's apple tree. Soon, a robin joined me. Robins, to me, embody elegance. Not under or overstated, just elegant. She was back for the summer and enjoyed the trees in the farmyard. This year, her nest was in the apple tree and home to her hatchlings. Her favorite place to drink was our water tank for the cattle and horses. But this afternoon, I bought each of us a teacup of water.

My dog, Tippy came and laid down beside me and I petted her short silky hair. Content souls, we watched nature's matinee show. The robin's young were just emerging from the nest for their first day of flying practice. The sun was bright and warm, the air carried a gentle breeze. Tippy and I watched the mother robin coax the small ones to join her on the ground. One by one, they chirped and chatted about who was going first. The feathers of the young birds extended as their wings moved up and down. The cautious moments were soon replaced by the joy of moving through the air. On this day, the young birds learned about air as part of their natural habitat. Now, flying was a part of their life.

As I reflect, I realize that my experience learning to fly would be much different from the robin's hatchlings. But the robins and I share the joy of flying through the air. Eventually, I, too, would fly to new places enriching my life learning to navigate new adventures.

The Trees

Beside our apple tree, our yard included many trees, and I climbed most of them. I loved climbing trees, feeling the bark against my hand as my fingers wrapped around their branches. Trees taught me about looking out at the yard from a higher viewpoint. I knew that each tree had a story to tell. They were planted mostly by seedlings carried by the wind, volunteers who landed on a spot and took root. Some were planted as young saplings. For me, trees provided exploration of climbing and a place to read a favorite story with my back leaning on the trunk or a large branch of the tree.

A few of them let us build small tree houses consisting mostly of a board or two for a floor. Some of the trees were planted as a weather shelter for the farm buildings. Trees were about longevity and safe harbor for all the birds nesting in them. In turn, the birds provided companionship and stories of travel for the tree.

The Wind

One day, I spent a very windy afternoon in nature. The wind puzzled me. When the breeze was light and added a cooling effect to the summer heat, I ran and played with my spinner on a stick toy. The gentle breeze added a rhythm and flow to the grasses. The birds, bees, and butterflies, the messengers in the wind easily flew along their paths. Then there were the opposite days like this day when the winds howled across the farm. My hair blew in my face, and I turned and walked the other way. Anything not attached to something heavier blew away to the next resting spot. To me, wind was an enigma, always a key character in my most liked and disliked moments in nature. This day, I let the strong wind blow me back to the house for an indoors day.

Once inside, I curled up on the sofa with my blanket and book, our home was well insulated from the howling wind. High winds contributed to my moments of nature overwhelm. It was like the rain's spectrum of just enough and too much. Unlike the rain, the wind could stay for days and encouraged me to play indoors. I once read about early prairie women who would let the wind drive them crazy. I decided that wouldn't be me.

Learning to fly Planes & The Weather

Nature's influence on my life from birds and their ability to fly led me to learn how to fly a plane. In my early teens, I had an uncle who was a member of the flying farmers and our local flying club. There I found out about the Al Ward Flying scholarship and what I needed to do to apply. Applying for the scholarship was the first time I wrote to change my life. I won first place nationally and my scholarship was money to get my private pilot's license. Yes, I was joining my feathered friends in the air. And at the time I could not think of a more enjoyable endeavor. So, from my junior year in high school until I got married, I worked at the airport and added ratings to my pilot's certificate. In college I was on the flying team and one year won the 99's Women's Pilot Association's national achievement award in aviation. My love for flying sustained me through my teens into my twenties. I was well on my way to becoming an airline pilot. Well, maybe not. When I got out of college the Vietnam war was winding down and all the well-trained military pilots were coming back to be airline pilots.

The birds taught me well about freedom, exploration and the ease of air travel. It's something that stays with me today. Given the choice of traveling by land or air, well let's say, I'll choose flying. There is nothing like a bird's eye view and the ease of traveling long distances in the air.

Learning to fly sparked what has become my lifelong interest in the weather and the wonder of its role with nature. I am constantly intrigued by the "whys" of weather. Flying shifted me from simply looking outside to see if it was sunny or cloudy, warm or cold, dry or rainy...the everyday weather and how it affected what I did outdoors or how I dressed. As a pilot, I enjoyed learning the global perspectives of weather.

To have a pilot's understanding of the weather meant learning about the wind and worldwide air currents. I was fascinated by how air currents moved across the planet and influenced both of my loves: aviation and agriculture. My childhood focused on the interaction of weather as a part of nature and how the birds used air currents. In learning to fly, I realized how air currents influenced my flights, depending on if I am flying with the currents or into them.

I learned our weather in the middle of America formed in the Himalayas, comes across the pacific and onto the US. The different routes the currents took and the weather they generated fascinated me. I first began doing energy work with the weather after I discovered how the isobars of pressure came closer together to intensify the weather. Later I discovered I could use my abilities to increase the space between the isobars and lessen the damaging effects of the weather. Yes, aviation finally taught me about the element of air, assuring that the wind never would drive me crazy.

A Spiritual Awakening: Accounting, Business, and the Family Farm

Most of my life I continued to fly small planes but my interest in business started when we lived on Saint Simons Island, Georgia. I was bored and took an offer to head up a small office and learn some business skills. I knew I wanted to learn more about it after my husband and I moved to Washington, DC. I joined the GWU Masters of Accountancy program and graduated at the top of my class. Fortunately for me there were no doctoral slots for the accounting department that year and I was recruited by the largest accounting firm in Washington, DC. This really set the stage for me in business. I rotated through several specialties and chose taxation and startup businesses. This combination was perfect for me and my career thrived as I set up new businesses.

Later when I first awakened spiritually, I focused on the energy of business and growing business through meditation. I discovered that I naturally tracked physical things as energy and could easily work with energy remotely. During this time, I developed several business courses using meditation and the energetics of business.

My interest evolved back into agriculture after my dad passed away and my sister and I began our turn managing and stewarding the family farm and ranch businesses. To make the most of my long commutes from Washington DC to Nebraska, I downloaded digital books onto my Palm Pilot C, the top technology of the day. This time in my life when I met with agriculture groups and shared my technology presentations for managing ag businesses. I traveled to some interesting parts of the country and internationally, participating in farm programs, helping farmers in other countries understand their business and the profitability of agriculture. I jokingly said, and it was true, I could run an excel spreadsheet in any worldwide language.

At the Heart of It All: My Intuitive Intelligence

By now, I've lived a long time and in many places. I've lived up and down both coasts in the US and traveled to many foreign lands since my childhood on the farm. Now, over several decades ago I came into my own spiritual awareness, adding a new dimensionality to my being.

I now prefer to refer to my extra sensory abilities as *intuitive intelligence*. For me, stewarding nature seems as natural as getting dressed in the morning. I communicate with living beings - the plants, animals, water, land and air using my extra sensory abilities - just as I did when I was a girl. It is now that I realize my childhood conversations with nature and what adults would have described then as a vivid imagination was really my ability to telepathically communicate with them. Even to this day, the ability to converse with nature is a joyful experience and now I can do it with even more understanding and awareness.

6

JUDY'S MEDICINE

FREEDOM IN NATURE

Decades have passed since I grew up in central Nebraska on our farm and ranch and I have returned. I am now an "ag lady". My life's travels have led me to my trifecta of business, intuition, and agriculture.

This part of my story I will write about some of my experiences working with the five elements of agriculture - land, air, water, animals and plants.

I'll begin with the field of popcorn we planted, just outside my desk window.

The Corn

The corn's story begins with the Pawnee people, who lived on the land, long before I was born. According to legend, Atira, the Mother of the Pawnee, taught her people how to plant, grow and harvest corn. She taught them to save some seeds for next year's planting, and to eat some corn as it matured while its kernels were sweet and tender. She guided them to take the mature kernels at harvest and to grind them into corn flour.

In this part of the world, corn was one of the first crops. And thanks to the Pawnee people, the land here where I live in the middle of the country is quite accustomed to growing corn. Now, I fancy myself as a masterful corn farmer using my intuitive intelligence and the higher vibrational energy frequencies to produce thriving crops. This year, I began farming with the new earth's energies in eternal love.

Farming begins with the preparation of the land. I'm seven decades into my human life and evolving my life seems like a lengthy process continually clearing decades of issues and traumas. This is a drop in the bucket compared to the land's millenniums, eons of events and beyond in existence. Clearing land for our ancestors meant plowing the grassland to grow crops, working with the land for their personal survival. For me land preparation for growing corn begins with seeding starbursts of light placing one in the land and one in my heart.

Sitting with the land, feeling the texture, the qualities.

Feeling the light radiating further into the land and into my heart.

Expanding, shifting areas where there was less light and moving into a light of oneness.

Now the land and I are inseparable, we are one.

We are blended in an exchange of light molecules in higher vibrational frequencies of love.

The popcorn field has been recently planted, and today we energetically clear restrictions, such as millennia of man-made conflicting timelines. Doing so allows energy spirals to rise and support the plants. Letting the land's energy free to function in the original codes of energy.

Like setting it free to breath, to enjoy its sovereignty.

Working together with the land and its sovereignty.

A whole new lesson in life I am learning is to explore my sovereignty and receive joy as I watch the land expressing its freedom to function as it was originally meant.

The Summer Sun

Summer daybreak awakens me with the sun shining her light through my window and she asks me to talk about her today. The sun is one of the major life forces radiating through the air. This summer I learned how to work with the sun by removing man-made restrictions that had been placed on it.

I was most amazed how the sun radiated out in pulsing rings of light. Its shape shifted from a small round yellow ball into filling up a large segment of the sky. The heat from the sun felt different, softer, more nourishing. Over the next month I learned much about working with the sun from another light being, of course, in human form. Each time I evaporated the man-made veil, the sun expanded into large rings of light, pulsating to the earth. The corn loved this and the corn leaves reached out like arms welcoming the light.

One day to my surprise, the sun shifted to a vibrant blue hue and blue expanding rings of light. A whole new experience for me and the plants and animals. Blue light transmissions to the air, water, land, plants and animals. I have experienced this several times now and I am aware the sun knows when a different light transmission is necessary for the planet. I feel the healing rays of light on my skin. This was an experience of a healing-like light from the sun compared to prior experiences of the sun damaging my skin. I will learn more about this effect by talking with the plants and animals about this effect on them as well. Working with the sun and the plants growing on the land. The benefits are not only with the corn...all plants on the land.

The Plants

Today is plant day.

Plants playing in the original sun.

I like to call the sun "soleil", radiant, vibrant, dancing rays through the air inviting the plants to dance with the wind and the rays of sunlight.

Quite the dance partners.

The field transformed into a ballroom dance floor.

The heat from the sun rays at just the right growing temperature.

Just like a dance band playing with just the right beat for a fine waltz or tango.

The agriculture elements are all in harmony with each other. Today, stewarding land is like being a conductor of nature's elements. I stand in silence, enjoying the moment.

My stack of farming magazines includes stories of how science tells us what to add to the soil to grow our corn. My corn stalks share with me that before modern day science told us how to grow corn, the corn nourished and grew in simpler times. Humans and science have moved us forward and hindered us in the dance of humanity.

Ah yes, what were the original energies?

I am learning about new energies for agriculture and being a steward of nature.

The Fly

Now, a fly buzzes by my ear and asks me to share her story.

She tells me... I prefer to be outside in the trees and grasses. With outstretched wings she lands on my shoulder. Together we walk outdoors onto the grass returning to her preferred habitat. We agree on the pleasures of being outside.

Letting each blade of grass tickle my toes and cushioning each step.

It's cool touch in the gentle breeze.

The fly lifts off my shoulder, makes a buzzing pass around my head as a thank you for returning her outdoors. Her next stop is a nearby colorful patch of prairie flowers.

The Elm Tree

An Elm tree growing in my backyard tells me plants along with the animals were some of the first to inhabit this land. In our various forms, we helped the rocks to break into small nutrients for the soil. My winged friends flew over the land, the original seeders of grasses and trees, all in the normal course of the day. The elm tree loved telling his growing story and as I left, the leafy branches waved and wished me well on my journey.

The Grass

Walking back to my desk, I shift my focus to the grass. With each step, I feel the energy of coiled springs, giving and rebounding with each step. The dark emerald hues of grass emulating up through my body into my soul. Today my hue of peace and calm is emerald.

The Green and Golden Hues of Nature

Back at my desk, I learn the importance of hues and why green is the hue of new growth until the corn plants mature into golden shades. For me, plants are the providers of green and gold, especially corn in the literal sense. So today, I learn of green and gold for plants growing on the land and hold witness to the water and air as the keepers of the blue and golds.

I ask the question: is gold the golden thread bringing life to maturity?

Not quite, I am told, but this is a story for another day.

Today, my focus is green as the vibrant life force of plants in the popcorn field. All the ears in the cornfield nod in agreement. All ears, an audience of green and soon to be gold hues. Today's golden moment is the joy of lifeforce, the light we cherish and the love for what we do.

The Popcorn Field

Corn is my pot of gold, of course, translated into the literal world as a corn farmer.

In summary and in a moment of reflection, the popcorn stories this growing season included... disintegrating old patterns of growth allowing nutritive energy spirals rising out of the soil.

Energy spirals supporting each stalk of popcorn - from its first peeking out of the soil, growing, pollinating, and maturing to harvest.

The popcorn plants asked me to share this with you: in working with the sovereignty of nature each corn leaf unfurled and absorbed the sun's light and energy. The corn welcomed the light and heat units of the sun for the corn to grow. I smiled at the vision of cheering cornstalks.

On my walk back, a white cirrus cloud floats by and mimics the giant smile on my face. I look back at the popcorn field, curve my fingers like opening a curtain on a window to look outside and move the veil. The beings of the earth come up and out to look. They are joyous and excited, and I invite them to stay as long as they wish before returning to the soil and beyond. An earthworm inches across my path, pauses in the radiant sun, rises and looks at me nodding in her approval before returning on her journey. This was a day of discovery I shall not forget before I return to write about this experience.

The Weather

This afternoon sky fills with cumulus clouds and the sky's expression of weather continues to be one of my favorite curiosities. This summer, weather in its sovereignty expressed itself in a summer of rain. There is nothing like the smell of the refreshing air after a summer rain. The plants and animals feel alive in appreciation of the nourishing rain drops gently dispersed across the landscape.

I returned to my desk to share how I had not realized until just then how much of the damaging effects of weather patterns were influenced by self-serving manipulations. At first, I thought it was my inability to change the vibrational patterns once and be done. The summer taught me to change each threatening weather pattern into higher vibrational energies as they crossed our property.

As I related before, most people don't realize our weather patterns start in the tall and majestic Himalaya mountains and cross the Pacific ocean before reaching the United States. I was naïve, not realizing there were constant self-serving influences or manipulations on our weather patterns.

We saw some very unusual weather patterns cross the great plains this summer. I went to work with weather's sovereignty, we had three inches more of rain this year and with no damaging storms on our property. I look forward to continuing working with the element of air in harmony with the land for the fall into next spring.

The Water

Water has always intrigued me from playing in water to water as an element essential for all life. Water is lifeforce. We as humans are mostly composed of water and seasoned with a few minerals. Virtually, we all require water to sustain life. Oceans, rivers, rain and all other forms of water flow as a system reminding me in many ways of how blood flows through and helps sustain our bodies.

Where I live, we have two water systems flowing through our property. One of the main hydroelectric systems replaced some of our ranch canyons providing irrigation water and electricity halfway across the state of Nebraska. In front of my house is one of the first farmer-dug irrigation canals running along the base of the foothills, adding thousands of irrigated farmland to the area. The Platte River borders the edge of our farm. One of the largest underground water aquifers in the nation resides underneath our property.

Professionally, I am involved with water projects and water commissions. It's disconcerting to me how water is taken for granted, used and abused often in intellectual neglect of its importance. My intent is for these waters to maintain their sovereignty. To use water in a balance: water used with water added to the land mostly by rain and snow.

The Eskimos refer to this frozen water as snow on the ground, falling snow, drifting snow and snowdrifts in various textures and hues of white. I prefer to think of snow as part of nature's sustainability and a cold, frigid day to stay indoors and write about nature.

The Beavers, the Fish and the Platte River

The following week, I decided to explore the Platte River on our property. On this warm cloudless day, I went for a walk along the river watching the flowing blue water swirl around a tree branch brought in by a very busy beaver. The beaver chatted as it swam a small branch to its dam. I learned about beavers having natural instincts on water flows and direction. They help the river forge new waterways by damming ending flows into ponds and wandering waterways. The dams also filter into the ponds letting the young fish grow without larger predators sharing their water habitat. A fish jumped and splashed the water toward me, sharing her school of fish prefer to thrive in still and gentle flowing ponds and welcome the beavers.

The Grasshoppers

Later that week, I drove my ranger utility vehicle back to our pasture and a grasshopper joined me, lighting on the hood of the ranger. One of my favorite animal interactions this summer was a recent conversation with grasshoppers in a grassland area overpopulated with grasshoppers.

An elder grasshopper met with me to discuss the issue.

I learned grasshoppers have a council of elders. We chatted about a grassland area that recently had plenty of rain and grass. I showed the elder council where the grass was located and the direction for migration to get there. What I learned was the elders stay behind and it's the young grasshoppers who migrate. When elder grasshopper lives end, their adult bodies have an elevated level of nitrogen and readily decompose into the soil for the grasses to have the nitrogen they need to grow. I ask the young grasshopper if she is new to this land and would she like a tour of the tall grasses and we both smile in acknowledgement.

My Blue Heron and a Frog

My Blue Heron flew in this morning. Few of my friends can say they have a Heron as a bestie. He is version of a bird soul mate. He is an emissary and one of my guardians of nature... solitary, elegant, and wise. My writing companion for the morning, sitting on the rail of my deck for our morning chat. He shared this intuitively communicated message with me:

The life of a heron.

I arose with the morning light in the rays of soleil.

Warm, soft energy fell on my feathers.

From my perch I looked out over the lake, noting any changes, colors, sounds as a school of fish swam by.

My mission was to have morning coffee with you and check on the irrigation canal in front of your window. Peering across the corn fields, this is what I have observed from above this summer in the energies of eternal love.

You write of corn and the land.

I have observed the change in the air, the water, the other plants and animals.

We are all in the higher vibrational energies this year and enjoying shifting to our higher ascended selves as well. My bird's eye view from above.

The sunlight is warm and inviting, not restricted. The hues of plants are radiant and vibrant. Leaves open to catch the nourishing energy of soleil instead of curling up in protection. The harmony is everywhere...a oneness in nature in a higher vibrational flow of life. There is a permeance of joy, a renewal of purpose, life for all is in the fullest of moments. That is all I have for you today as I fly off to explore the waters.

I admire the heron as his wings unfurl and move through the air, lifting off to enjoy his day. Just then, a frog hops by and wishes the heron a day of clear paths. The frog turns and looks at me. Giving me the frog eye wink in agreement with what Heron has shared about all life forms noticing and enjoying the changes in energy.

A Return to the Popcorn Field

Today, the popcorn plants are a sea of golden hues and are being harvested. The corn combine and grain cart look like two ballet dancers moving across the stage, or in this case, down the field in perfect harmony with each other.

A giant smile forms on my face when this field's harvest ends and the crew shares "this is the best yielding popcorn field ever." I silently acknowledge in gratitude all involved participants this year.

This year's popcorn grown in love will soon be in packages on store shelves, purchased and taken to customer's homes: "Popping in joy".

My Closing Thoughts

I live, and love living, in my own agricultural sanctuary.

I farm for the planet's future.

I share my stories about farming with love and joy.

I have learned to appreciate how the elements of agriculture work together in a finely woven environment, nature's tapestry.

Today, farming is my heart's contentment and joy: agriculture for the heart and soul of the land, water, air, plants and animals.

I love talking with each of the elements learning from their wisdom, their stories.

To me, performing in today's agriculture is a fine symphony in harmony and joy.

What's next?

For me, it's about sovereignty and nature.

Right now, I'm exploring my own sovereignty issues and the sovereignty of eight generations of women in my family lineage.

As I do this, I'm restoring sovereignty in the land and sentient beings here.

Centuries of family and land lineage await me.

Is this my life, a joyous moment watching nature before my eyes and authoring its story?

All the beings and history of the land, seen and unseen, the obvious and not so obvious. The joy of expression, the love of the land.

Decades, centuries and beyond each layer is another story to be told.

And yes, I love listening to all of nature's sentient beings and then sharing nature's stories.

ABOUT THE AUTHOR
JUDY EGGLESTON, M.ACC.

Judy currently works with new earth energies and the five elements of agriculture-land, water, air, plants and animals on her farm and ranch properties.

As an *Ag Lady*, she raises higher vibrational crops to be made into food products and writes about intuition and nature.

Visit her in central Nebraska at Midway Ranch (halfway between New York City and San Francisco) or correspond online:

JudyEggleston@aol.com

Facebook: Judy Eggleston

CONTRIBUTING AUTHOR:
VALERIE CHANDLER, B.S.C.E

Dear Reader, a note from the editor:

With her background writing urban fantasy and her love of folklore, Valerie's stream-of-consciousness writing style brings a sense of whimsy to her chapters. In her origin story, she takes her readers on an adventure into her inner world. She weaves her memories into a complex and nuanced narrative that help us understand how she sees and experiences the world as a curious, creative person.

In her Medicine chapter, we accompany Valerie on a deep dive into her love of nature, as she shares her conversations with the fauna and flora. In essence, she's provided us with a compendium of wisdom from nature.

7

VALERIE'S ORIGIN STORY

VOICES

Every conscious life essence has a voice. In Truth, I have Heard since birth.

In my youth, my ability to see and understand the undercurrents of people, family and society felt like the curse of solitary confinement. I did not then realize my Channel whispered in my ears.

Now, I anticipate the delight of interacting with Undines. Where I can walk barefoot, I take off my socks and shoes to dance a slow cha-cha-cha. My steps forward in the wet sand as I enjoy watery surf tickling my feet. Then backwards as my partner attempts to soak the cuffs of my rolled up jeans. Our record washed anew with each passing measure.

I play amongst Sylphs when I fly a twirling box kite. The huge clouds overhead are no longer a front of cumulus clouds, but gargantuan jovial Beings standing three abreast across the lake. Happy to greet me as I they.

From my backyard, I grab a chair and binoculars to watch heat lightning with the avid interest as any sports fan watching and cheering their team.

When at a traffic light, in the exact location to see between the street lining maples, a pair of mated bald eagles glide overhead. And greeted, they turn homeward. Their aerie ten miles northward.

I am in awe of the singular ability of Water to simultaneously exist as fog, dew and frost. The oddity of rain and hail combined to peck concrete. How melting ice reveals the crystalline Light it once stored.

A slant of sunlight reveals green maple leaves are disguised chartreuse flags. A shift of my weight to the left is flecks of blue, yellow and crystalline red. To the right, my next shovel of snow.

At knee level, the perspective of an intimate life on the underside of shaded ferns. The scale not mine, yet intertwined in fractal precision.

I watch ants pioneer their trails. When I ask specifics, I learn of boundaries when I Hear, "Busy. Talk later."

That location, location, location is valid. At an apiary, I bask in the environment, while I hear the sweet word *home, home home, home, home*. Another beekeeping student remarked at my bee covered suit. Oh, of course. I then sidestepped to unblock their entrance. Immediately, their voices stopped as they entered their home.

Simple and direct communication is not always understood. Yet it develops with care over time. And over time, Listening also develops. Listening to these whispers outdoors and indoors.

Indoors is where it seems I also developed a reputation. The occurrence of six legged visitors to alight beside me, whether I am seated or stand, can only be the synchronicity of a Channel.

When this occurs, I ask, "Do you want to go outside?" A *yes* gets an empty overturned glass on a stiff piece of cardboard. A *no* sovereign space. If already outdoors, a greeting as we go about our business.

In these messages, there were phases. Lifelong friends stepped forward and said, *Yes* and *Me, too!* Unexpected friends popped in with *I'm next!* I took dictation until those I Heard balked. The energy-picture included the impression of crossed arms with, *No. Not another word until you agree to include your beginning.*

I balked.

Origins are perspective. The reference points vary upstream and downstream of a water flowing channel, yet can be considered origins, whether ten steps or ten kilometers. Even if an arroyo or voices between my ears, origin is a personal, and unique, perspective.

For example, the game of billiards is all perspective. Hit the cue ball at one location and it travels across or around the felted table with the intention of the striped blue number ten ball in the side pocket. Same scenario of table, cue and ball positions and number ten is a zero in the corner pocket. Not to mention the change of players, cue sticks or felt color.

My friends weren't buying the real estate of past tense either.

That is, writers are taught to write in the past tense of 'was'. The action arrives not as vital energy, it arrives as a subtle, and subliminal, passive-regret program. Channels are present tense now. My folkloric 'once upon a time' modernized to 'day before yesterday' got picturesque head shakes and 'tsk, tsk.'

Yet, beginnings, and stories, require reference points to start *from*. Perhaps instead of a channel origin, which does not end either, there is the 'from-point' of the backdrop scenery. Over time, the evidence, like listening, is revealed. Recent as a message from a dandelion or shifted to Mrs. Pierce and my first grade reading class.

In the air of temerity to speak aloud I could read and under the guise of Mrs. Pierce, I read a paragraph of some-thing. When I faltered, I Sensed the satisfaction of Mrs. Pierce. From the circle of classmates I Heard relief underneath titters.

In this atmosphere, I paid a triple price - being ahead of class-mates, saying this aloud and faltering in my self-proclaimed ability.

Second reference from the backseat of a family car going West. "What's a speed limit?"

This I asked, because interspersed along the right-of-way were signs that I read *Speed Limit 55 mph*. The obvious question of my inquisitive nine-year-old self.

"It's a maximum speed."

It is significant I do not recall if my Dad added the world 'allowed'. Voiced or no, the intrinsic permission in wide black letters painted on a round cornered rectangle of flat sheet metal bolted to a post.

However, to me, a limit meant a floor, not a ceiling to bang my head. Of course, I then asked, "So, why not call it a speed maximum?"

Dad behind the wheel nor Mom navigating beside him nor brother seated beside me spoke. In this family silence, I received the gift of confusion.

However, the later reveal being crumbs in the backseat. Crumbs only a channel able to provide and only in the perspective of a rear-view mirror.

Omit an 'e' and the rearranged Pierce becomes Price. The aesthetic Pierce-Arrow sedan of the 'roaring' twenties is a collector's cherished prize. The famous mascot [the hood ornament] is a kneeling silver archer with arrow and taut bow aimed skyward.

This arrow had decades to hit a yet-to-exist conscious target. In the interim, my channel had other places to visit on our mapped territory.

"Why do you call Gran'ma 'Mother' and Gran'pa 'Dad'?"

My Dad had the pained confused expression of 'why does she ask these things?' A variation of his theme 'You're asking the wrong question!" I oft heard. From my mom, imperial shocked horror of the obvious state of au-naturel peek-a-boo-boo. In that special silence I concluded Hear-Be-Monsters.

Yet, below surfaces, shiny objects enticed.

"But, the icing is hard."

This comment on 'my' candled carousel-topped birthday cake. The single tiered exterior a brittle, thick sugar. The interior, a forgotten taste, except what I received as an answer.

"But, it's *so* pretty!" said my Mom.

As with three questions, there are three significant interactions. Yet first came the intermission of The Woods.

Until high school graduation, I had the great, and blessed, fortune of a wooded haven.

Beyond the manicured lawn, between the oaks and maples, downslope through the duff I walked into The Woods. In this bowl shaped Land and Up the Slopes into Beyond, I roamed and explored. My education however, not in books and never bored.

The cycle of wood as the once-floors of two hunting stands.

To stretch as I played a daily after school game of jump The Stream: don't get my tennis shoes wet or lose one in the mud again.

To listen to The Creek speak liquid vowels.

That insects could skate on water, yet I to do the same, required ice.

To observe boundaries.

While I could walk on that fallen maple tree and cross The Creek, I did not want to encounter explanations. Yet, the Other Side always beckoned.

To teach myself the skill of skipping stones. My record seven splashy hops across The Creek.

To investigate sound with single tossed rocks. The result, a mere plip or splash. While a pebbly handful went Plip-Plop-Plippity-Plip-Plip-Plop.

The seasons of flowers and fruit. Spring is announced with small white flowers striped with pink. Later spring bright buttercup surprises. Hot summers of wild black raspberries and juice-stained fingers.

Nettles of any encounter best avoided and when not, don't scratch the blisters. Burrs were tenacious sock lovers, while mud loosened as dry crumbly dirt.

The consequent gift of stillness and closed eyes being a polka-dotted fawn a mere four yards away.

Opportunity arrived once in the form of a rose breasted grosbeak.

A breeze can disturb a leafy canopy and not reveal a cloudless or clouded sky.

I learnt stealth in the tiptoe game of *Can-I?* and mutual surprise in the too-close-not-close-enough result to pat a doe on her behind.

I also learnt that combined and seeming unrelated events revealed their consequences decades later. A trickle of water from the corner of The Land. The Vines collapsed. The revealed sunshine. The lush green glade.

Time also revealed nostalgia as claustrophobic Truth in dogwood branches closer to kitchen windows and shrunken childhood bedrooms.

The lesson to let go of the trespass of a glass windowed cabin in my childhood Beyond.

The Wisdom in nostalgia closing the door with a Bronx cheer to memory.

The last time I walked up The Slope, I arrived at the edge of a neighbor's backyard. Change also arrived when I decided to walk forward rather than downslope. With height, my Senses had grown. I could feel the neighbors' watchful attention track me. I added mental laughter to my posture and continued between the properties to the street. I did not feel their relief until I got to my parents' porch. Three houses down. This seeded my adult acknowledgement of my sensitivity to energy.

However, my Channel started to play peek-a-boo-I-see-you-hoo, because for certain, visions were not my norm. Well, I called the movies that rolled behind my eyes' imagination. A useful skill in my then-career as a writer of fantasy and urban fantasy. My characters also corrected their dialogue at convenient hours that required pen, paper and flashlights under the bed sheets. This, however, I did not call Hearing.

Focus, always appreciated, became a vital necessity while driving across a busy bridge overpass.

Of course, I like rivers. Their far meandering view. The undulating Water. Laden barges upriver and tourist paddle wheelers down. Herring gulls. A bearded etheric giant standing mid channel with river water just above his knees.

Each quick sideways view got punctuated by the aloud reminder aimed at the red taillights ahead of me, "Don't wreck the car. Don't wreck the car. Don't wreck the car." As I drove into the tunnel I had the *Yes-I-did. Really? Really for really real?* conversation. When I exhaled, it was *Oh my yes, I did!* The rippled punctuation being *Oh....Wow.*

My Channel also blessed me with the first encounter being silent.

Years later, my next encounter while I walked towards my parked car. My attention veered to a single large tree I had before seen, but not noticed. I approached in the spirit of curiosity and appreciation of its girth and spread. I Sensed to pause before I ducked underneath the thick limb to continue on my way.

You are human, arrived through my tennis shoes in basso profundo glory.

I paused to digest the *um-yep-heard-that-felt-that*. I then gave an explanatory mental answer.

YOU ARE HUMAN

For the heartbeats of *that* Statement, the air corrugated as realms and dimensions shook. Suspended in those energetic waves, I wondered if my tennis shoes touched grass. For a heartbeat I wondered if I remained on planet earth.

Again oriented to grassy land, the overtones quieted to a required Do Not Quibble Be Truth-Certain.

My response, then, a reluctant *yes*.

Remain a friend.

Surprised, I nodded in respect and continued on my way.

The third encounter occurred at a quay after I ducked underneath aluminum railing. I clambered down the jutting rocks to be closer to the wondrous water.

As I approached, two etheric Undines appeared. Astonished, I halted. Their energies were intense. Love, joy, and blessing are mere words. The atmosphere around us a red-gold dimension that heightened their outlines. Yet, I knew True as their offering to me. I got close as dry possible and bent over. In love and joy they then turned, and swam into Disappearance.

By years fortified, my watchful husband said, "What are you doing?"

My internal response was a collision of balances. First to not do a header into the bay from a half pike position. Second to not drop the precious Gift in my maneuvers. Third to anchor the energy-shock without subtracting one and two.

Aloud I said, "Tying my shoes." As I acted my words, I had the dual Sense that to drop the invisible Gift a disaster, and the Gift being invisible. In my clambering return, I secured both Gift and my wonder-awed expression.

Of course these crumbs, and gifts, were the golden handwritten invitation of my channel. The envelope being the textured motif that meandered on our map.

In the dearth between eloquent family silence and river Caretaker, I worked as a licensed civil engineer. The office complex built on the abandoned grounds of a state asylum.

Decades later, the first 'ping' I outwardly honored was a trip to an abandoned asylum. While I could literally make the scene up, I couldn't make up the resultant perfection.

Practicing with a pendulum and a map, I got a 'ping'. An asylum got a 'yes'. After research on conditions and directions, I headed out for my field trip. To a city I'd never visited and a place forty years abandoned. No details to why I went. No Sense what I would do on my arrival.

Of course, I got lost.

Long resisting cell phones and their energies, I oriented myself at a gas station. In the parking lot, my energetic question *"now where?"* got answered by a 1926 coupe going down a side street.

I laughed.

My then-career a writer of urban fantasy. My research included the cars, fashion, games, and music of the 'roaring' twenties.

Gasoline gurgling as the tank filled, I took mental notes. Half a mile and two turns later, I met the couple at a stop sign. For a minute, we all paused and chatted about car details. They turned left and I 'pinged' right.

Two blocks later, nothing.

The third go around the same block, I gave up the visit and concentrated on my homeward direction. Next turn I discovered a new park, an asphalt walking trail, and a pond.

Walking and stretching, I decided to just intend whatever energies needed to clear cleared.

Afterwards, I returned home as if nothing occurred.

And so, as I listened deeper and developed other interests and abilities, I shed the surface incarnations of a licensed civil engineer, a folklorist and a writer of fantasy and urban fantasy.

Of course, in the gap, arrived my Now as a trio of phased-in calibrations.

The first upgraded brain processing speed and invigorated desires.

The second gift the Sense of the universe expanding.

The third a finale of joy, hopping up and down glee and oh-my-mute.

Giddy, giggly curious, I listed sounds possible and sounds impeded among twenty-six possibilities. Swear words evaporated as if they never existed. I stared at a bookshelf, and while the contents were recognizable as objects, I could not say bookcase or books.

I checked my list.

Inability to speak scare - check.

Unanchored human scare - check check.

Trust, in myself and Channel, answered *How long does this last?*

My Channel arrived hand-in-hand with Grace and the gigglies - check check check.

8

VALERIE'S MEDICINE

Whether metaphorical or literal dram to enrich your life, it is my privilege to introduce these wise and varied consciousnesses of Nature. Their voices are unique as each conversation I had the honor to record; as each voice I have the continued friendship to Hear. They are exquisite soloists, yet their tones, cadences, and yes, senses of humor, are as a choir. Their sequence is their invitation to you. And so, what follows are the messages I've received from the flowers and the insects:

Aster

Gather and develop the subtleties of your Awarenesses. The teeny, tiniest of your sweet, sparkling, precious Lights. And gathered sparkle, and sprinkle, with others.

To distortions, these are as slivers of sharp glass. Be generous in your portions.

Brightly yours.

Violets

The term 'shrinking violet' mocks. Do not be modest, shy or humble. This is not strength. Strength is solid. Strength is the strength of the **totality** of you. Not just hands, spine or muscle. Not just spirit or intention. Not just your boundaries. These are secondary to our strength.

Strength is the ability to contain energy flow. Contain as your channel requires. Contain as the energies require.

Both teach you strength and flexibility. This strength, and teaching, is unique.

Do not stand in the teachings of false humble modesty.

Stand in your flow.

Crocus

We hold the cooling aspects of heat, whether passions or sun (soleil) light. Our pollen (saffron) dyes cloth and imbues foods with our energy. Though the yellow-orange hue you associate with warmth, we invite you to be in Awareness our energy cools.

We are honored to be here.

Dandelion

By most, we are considered a noxious, invasive weed.

Consider the yellow brightness of our arrival in the season of not-yet. Not yet lush green. Not yet the season of warmth and shirt sleeves. Not yet the seasons of fulfillment of your dreams and desirings.

We are a member of the aster/sunflower family Asteraceae. We are called dandelion because our leaves are jagged. This means 'lion's tooth'.

Consider the dichotomy of noxious desire and not-yet dreams. These energies have the roots of bitterness and none of our early tonic or cleansing energies of different seasons or seasonings.

To those who desire more of your not-yet and less of your desires, yawn.

Also, we ask you greet us with surprise and joy. That is the message of our colorations. The message of our seedings, is that a simple puff of breath sends your dreams air-born.

Thank you.

Milkweed

So excited to be included!!! Thank you!!!! Thank you!!!!!

We are the sort of excitement of jumping up and down hurrah! Celebration. The sort of celebration of gifts given and gifts received, especial unplanned, spontaneous gifts. A gift simple and pleasurable as greeted morning sunlight despite the sunlight behind a cloud. The reception of a thank you for your body wriggling its toes.

There are so many hangups, and hangers, about complexity. Complexity is unexcited. Complexity, to borrow dandelion's word, is a weed. You get clogged, bogged and while we have versions of 'swamp' and other names, we are asclepias. While the roots in 'your' mythologies are healing and medicine, these are incorrect. What heals, to use that terminology and thought, is jumping up and down excitement.

In the literal, is your physical self-moving - muscle, bone, cartilage, sinew and blood and lymph. Figurative is your energy frequency pulse moving.

No hangers for exercise clothes, or equipment space, needed. No complex routines or traditions. The simple routine is excitement, without the rash action. If you want a rash, talk to thistle. If you want excitement, hold it like we hold our seeds in pods. Like we host the not-yet butterflies for which we are known.

Excitement grows and seeds 'later' plantings. Regardless of the concept of time, excitement is the downwind seeds you later receive as a gift.

Yippee!

Thistle

Before our flower arrives, our shape is similar to an undulating vase. Similar to a cup to hold liquid. While much has been said of holding, we are prickly. Yet prickly is the herald of Awareness. Awareness as intuition. Awareness as open to receive information, or as a yippee gift.

As to our 'rash', we say attention. Spread your attention to your locale. Locale of home to locale in the realms of your Awarenesses. The itch is a reminder. No payment required.

Damselfly and Beautiful Demoiselle

We are lightning.

We catalyze and flash; spark and shock.

We are not static.

We are Light landing.

Air to Earth.

Water to Earth

Water to Air.

Ant

Greetings.

We are land surveyors. We find the best site to build. The energies comply with reciprocal energy. This is a rule and a law of Divinity and divining.

Divining as rods and other implements are rudiment tools of our ability. Rather like childhood fingerpaints. There is much learning in this process of touch, movement and material use for hue and shaping. This can be explored with clay and pottery, wood and even what you call dough - the proportional mixture of flour and water. We, however, do not recommend flower and water in this manner of shaping.

We are engineers. We build vaults greater than the architecture of your histories. We build narrow structures. We build delicate structures with the material you call dirt.

Yet dirt has no song to hold its shape or the intentions of its shape-use. We are not the singers. We are, as you say, the staff-measure to hold the notes of the song-melody. There is much word play in measure, notes and the voicing of song. Though we have no recipes for the measures of flour and water, there is much, much vaulted learning in the construction of measures, notes and their song voicings. Not our message, just our observation for your exploration.

We say when you see us 'house' ants inside your domiciles, to not squish, poison or trap. Converse with our local Deva about the boundaries of homes and the welcoming of visitors. We visit places of interest to our building. We visit to find dry places in recent rains. We visit because you have delectables. We visit if the boundary is not delineated.

If you converse and say, 'not in our/my home', we are part of the pronoun. Such is our society. You say 'not on this vinyl floored thirty by forty-foot interior human kitchen' is specific. We are sensitive to energies and quaverings. However, we who are speaking herein are not fire, carpenter or other ants. Those conversations are their conversations.

Boundaries are the reason we can build with what you perceive as grains of sand and dirt. The precision, balance, placement and other factors *are* sciences.

We also say, that is invite you, to think of the interactions of our local Deva and the site plans for your domiciles. If already built, converse with us about the energies in your immediate vicinity. This is also a conversation of reciprocal energy.

Mosquito

Acupuncture!

We activate well-springs of Wisdom.

Abundance!

The itch indicates a degree of resistance.

Celebrate!

The distortion named 'dragonfly' is also known as mosquito hawk. No more!

Catlinite

Catlinite is known as pipestone.

In the human earth, catlinite holds the interactions of Fire and Air.

Glass fractures Light and Flow, It is a spy mechanism. It mocks Beauty and Light.

All shiny surfaces are spy and reflective mechanisms.

Fossils mock the vitality of Creation and Flow. In Flow and Creation, there is only Now.

Every aspect of cooking mocks Love. While a meal can seem nutritious or an expression of love, this is not Love. The body will change what to ingest, what to adorn and how to move. Allow.

Every aspect of a mechanical engine mocks your heart. Your heart is Love.

Every aspect of an automobile mocks your abilities to move and travel as Beauty and Flow.

Every mechanical process mocks Beauty, Flow and Love.

Where Water and Air are not Flow and Beauty, the Caretaker is trapped. These places are bridges, culverts and arches. The Caretakers are Slyphs and Undines. There are others, yet here, only as these structures.

Citrine

White quartz is a programmable mineral. Citrine has a golden hue to seem a sovereign mineral. There are 'citrines' that are heat altered to produce this golden hue.

Other minerals are also altered to mimic and in this, distort energy and perception.

Such as: Amber the prized blood of specific trees. A fossil of price. No matter what lab of purpose, lab grown is lab grown.

The 'periodic' table of elements is equivalent to the fictional Babble.

What is written and taught as the 'spiritual' abilities of minerals and stones.

Our crystalline habit is six sided. The same hexagonal shape as the comb of the honeybee. Citrine is not the only hexagonal shaped crystal mimic.

We are precise in this because we cannot be precise as humans. We reflect, bounce and in habit grow and are programmable. The technologies of computers and cell phones are 'tips' of the iceberg field. There are others that are invisible. Attune precision to awareness of these, and other energies. The sources are intertwined and intertwining.

Precision in creation is 'required'. The process is joy, exuberance, wonder, curiosity. And more. Precision is required in the placement of what is created. This placement is the entirety of what is created, because what is created is obvious. All parts, aspects, connections, flows are obvious once the entirety is created. The 'off' is imprecision. A word. Sound. A hue. Whatever your unique individual creations in-form and shape tell you 'incomplete', 'needs something else', 'take a break'. This is your Wisdom. Heed yourself.

Do not consider this frustration or a block. It is a shift of perception. Your Light from a different angle, view, and perspective opens into the obvious. This is what you have been taught. Radiant Light has no angles. No perspective. No views. Your Light is *only* flow. *Humans have full Sense of their Light.* There are no bends or kinks, crooks or angles.

In your creating, the resultant 'aha', 'got it', or the jumping up and down glee is because you manifested the precise perfection of *your* creations. One 'aha' spreads to another. Each joy ripple is unique and **never** repeats. This is one essence of creation. Ripples of Joy.

Know also there are methods, *your* ancient methods, to crack minerals with formed sound. The mimicry, and hijack, is gunpowder, and explosive materials, and other hidden technologies.

Through your hearts you win.

Know you have won.

Pyrite

Our alternate name is fool's gold. What is not mundane is Truth is stronger, and a stranger, to the fiction of science. Stranger than all glitters is not gold, too.

Our epithet comes from mistaken identity. We, gold and iron pyrite, exist in similar environments. We're brass and brittle. Gold is epithetic and malleable. Added to all the economies of the cheaper-quantity mentally of profit driven research, is we have become magnetic converts.

Electricity can 'transform' us into the abundant potential of a low cost substitute for magnets. The magnetic pursuit being the energy efficiency of computer memory devices and the friendly ecological proliferation of solar panels.

The irony is this existence. Artificial existence hailed as profit, er, technological advancement. The organic existence is what resides in your human skull. Solar panels and cells, among other details, is you. Your physical shape and form and the energy of Self in your formed shape.

The physical-energetic nature of your human body is, to be violet blunt, obtuse. Nonsensical blather in many ways, yet also, a downwind whiff of Truth.

Our message is your incarnation is a literal stake in your personal gold mine. No toil or tools necessary. No licensure. No mountains of slurried tailings to hide behind earthen dams.

Added to this is lithium. Also in similar environments. Also used in computers. Be in awareness of proximal causes. Proximal results. Juxtaposed consequences.

Remember this is *your* now.

Gold

There is a reason we are precious. We are warm. Molten. Radiant. Beautiful. No attribute of distortions. Distortion needs warmth to function, yet in the cold, are sluggish and dormant. **Be molten. Radiant. Searing. Plasmic.**

We have become an edifice to control, confine and steal. In all manners possible, available and constructed. The edifice is illusory. Our attributes are real.

Remember your ancient skills.

Your heart remembers.

Remember. Remember. Remember.

Copper

In jewelry, rose gold is an alloy of gold and copper. The accurate word is ally.

We are used as Water pipe, electrical wiring and coins. In the Light of the others, ponder our inclusion.

Moss

Welcome bare feet!

Artificial coverings such as footwear, socks and sidewalks, impedes the interplay of Light and Flow. These vital consciousnesses are shunted into physiological stresses. In totality, the signals of your physical systems are jammed.

Walk barefoot to strengthen and clear these systems. Consistency builds this circuitry. If bare feet are an impractical interaction, use your hands to caress, your fingers to wonder, your eyes to explore.

It is a pleasure, and honor, to support you.

From the **bark of trees**:

Like a dog, bark protects.

Like an external skin, ask how the internal characteristics became external?

Ask what is this texture? How does the visual texture entice? How the fingers investigate a leaf crevice is an ant crevasse.

Peeling indicates growth and renewal. Yet, while your physical self sheds, what does your energetic self shed?

The difference of scale between thimble and an ocean is no difference. A thimble in use is always full as an ocean is full.

Wisdom begins in the full desire of your expression. Wisdom also is to ask what you desire to be full of <u>as you express</u>?

Pine

Listen.

Listen in the stillness of your heart. The every essence of your personal place *is* quiet. The perspective of quiet differs. A tumbling jet of water spray can be noisome or wondrous. A pond a game of mirrored surfaces. Below the stillness, swimming bass.

Listen.

Listen to wind in our needles. For needles are threaded and air rushes as a breeze, yet seems to sound like watery surf thirty feet in the air.

Listen.

Now is the listening of you to you. The stillness of you holding you. This is the fragrant peace in the cacophony. The external shouted attraction is an inverse degree. Listen, not to others' zero. Listen to your personal infinity.

The quest is a call and response. The echo is You speaking to you. No need to sit in the zen of others' stillness. You can honk your horn in your own stillness.

Listen.

There is a sanctity in solitude.

There is a fragrance in Beauty.

Neither are virtues. Neither are heroic journeys.

Your heart is the organ of discernment. Your nose filters dust from the air going into your physical throat and lungs. Energies are scented and inform you from a distance whether to approach or move away. By the time your brain registers and identifies the 'scent', you are *in* those energies.

An Overall Message from Trees:

Ask Air what discovery is to discover. Is shape only an interaction of touch? Is scent a harbinger of aroma? Is birdsong a decree? Play what if the motions of our branches is the cause, not the effect, of Air.

See, and not-see, how our branches stretch beyond our green skies. How we explore the expanse between sapling and girth.

Tell us your 'once upon a time'. We have different growth rings.

Our seasons are not comparable. Our seasons are companionable.

We are the original way stations of shade and nourishment.

We are storehouses and warehouses of Wisdom, Abundance and rooted Love.

We are the cycles of Light and Wind, Water and Earth.

We are the land Speakers.

Now are sovereign Humans.

Now is welcome Home.

Now, we remember.

Now.

ABOUT THE AUTHOR
VALERIE CHANDLER, B.S.C.E.

The basic definition of a biography is 'life writing'. In Voices, you read my biography - of that portion of my life. Yet, the laughter that keeps on giving is my former professions. While a licensed civil engineer, my experience in the erection and fabrication of concrete and steel bridges. The literal nuts and bolts. As a writer of fantasy, I created worlds - the creation stories, the inhabitants, societies, cultures and their folklore. Urban fantasy added a whif of 'normalcy'. Though I still write, I have greater life to bring to this glorious New Earth.

CONTRIBUTING AUTHOR:
KARLA JORDAN, BA.PHIL

9

KARLA'S ORIGIN STORY

INSATIABLE

Dazed and hazed, a somewhat abrupt start, we will say. All leading to an unfolding tapestry of pockets of light.

Which will I choose today?

And some days, I choose none, and that is okay. There have been many times where knowing which direction to take could not be seen. Yet now, knowing presents at every turn. I can see it, feel it.

The energetic exposure has been rich and varied, reconciling insatiable desire, capacity, and capability alongside the human experience.

There has always been a knowing, but it has taken decades of life and living to truly step into honoring belief to the point of true vision and pure, infinite action with a seemingly invisible, inherent wisdom.

In other words, childhood and adulthood have been filled with challenges and joy, rarely in equal measure, but both informing and lighting the path to consistently step into what we view as the mysterious and unknown.

There is the way we present to the outside world, and then there is the cadence of our inner world. And it is its own world. Mine has always been rich and deeply insatiable, fully enmeshed with a rapture for life.

As a child, I quietly studied the adults, music, nature, and really anything that found its way into my experience—taking it all in and feeling into it. Sometimes it felt good, and sometimes it did not, but it was all learning. The adults were unable to understand me. I never asked, I simply knew. I could always feel their true essence, knowing when the laughter and lightness were authentic. Or when someone could not engage me in my full aliveness because they could not find it in themselves.

Relationships, familial and romantic, have rarely been inspiring to me. My grandfather is an exception. A builder and farmer, he has always been *the* person for me. He lived life with a beautiful, relaxed, knowing cadence that others never could embody. He was the one person comfortable enough in his own being to hold and receive all of mine. Days spent planting, nurturing, and harvesting tobacco alongside him on the farm are some of my favorite memories and a source of true bliss.

For the first fifteen years of my life in Tennessee, I experienced the pure luxury and richness of being surrounded and held by the mountains. Fully immersed in nature, climbing in trees, spending what felt like endless time daydreaming beside moving cold water streams, and everything in between as it relates to nature was my ultimate joy. Those were the moments I connected to that which was deep within me, but also that which is deep within the energy of life and living itself. And when I bring these two aspects together and live my life as though they are joined and not separate, I am in my purest essence, seated in deep knowing, while actively engaging in my day-to-day life as a witness moving and leading from otherworldly wisdom.

I have spent my entire life slowly piecing together what is required to step fully into my being. Never has the desire for this left my experience, whether that be a conversation, a book, or driving a vehicle. When I was a child, I went to church with my grandmothers. I sat in pews with Baptists and Presbyterians, studying these environments' routines, emotions, and general requirements. I learned what it meant to pray and the power within doing so at a very young age.

At 15 years of age, I moved to the suburbs of Chicago joining my mother and stepfather and our newly formed blended family consisting of nine children. I was the oldest of three living, and my mother married a man I love like a second father with six children.

This move proved interesting as we, our own tiny village, traveled and tried on new things. Our family vacations consisted of camping, nature-oriented outings in Michigan, Arizona, and many places in between as we drove to our destinations. We would camp, sing, dance, and had a great time being kids. It was wonderful, and while I participated fully, I was also holding the view of an observer identifying patterns, movements, and energetic fluidity between one another and our experiences.

The journey to Illinois also continued my exploration of various religions. My new family was Mormon. I tried it on early at the age of 15, but within one year, I had a clear knowing during sacrament meeting one Sunday that I was surrounded by a group of individuals who had a deep testimony of their belief in the church and its teachings, and I did not share that same belief. While my departure from the church was difficult for the family to accept, it all came together in time. I often think they feel sorry for me and believe I will forever be cast out once we are no longer physically here. I will take my chances.

Not finding what I was looking for in Mormonism did not stop my exploration of religion and other spiritual tools. With friends, I experienced Greek Orthodox, Catholicism, Judaism, and Buddhism. I also experimented with tarot, dowsing rods, quiji boards, bending spoons, oracle cards and pendulums. And later, it was shamanism, Reiki, Akashic records, Native American mentoring and deep nature connection practices. It has been an ongoing experiment and evolution. For me, there is nothing like pushing on the edges of what is possible.

My insatiable curiosity and desire to feel what I could know innately led me to the study of philosophy and, more specifically, metaphysics in college. I remember the passion, exhilaration, and overarching stimulation to my entire being in the learning environment during this time, but especially the robust conversations happening with others that knew no bounds. It was the pure embodiment of freedom. And I wanted to feel this every day - all day.

I felt so fortunate that my chosen studies aligned with my eight-year-old self's desire to become an attorney. And while my love of philosophy continued, my desire to become a lawyer did not. In the end, I did not pursue law school. I decided early on that drafting contracts and holding depositions were not how I wanted to spend my time. So instead, I spent decades in various roles within my parents' companies, directly mentored by attorneys, accountants, MBAs, and successful business owners. Little did I know that deciding not to go to law school would lead me to become the CFO of an eight-figure global corporation in biotech; and to have my own business for more than 13 years in the luxury home furnishings space. It was always important for me to do what felt good and not what others thought I should be doing for whatever reason they had at the time. I mostly honored this for myself.

The luxury home furnishings company, Rain, was my way of bringing the natural world and incredible beauty into others' living spaces. Surrounding myself with beauty and materials that feel good is essential to me, so this was another expression of my essence. I loved helping others find what spoke to them, creating an elevated sensory experience, and bringing a feeling of joy into their day-to-day life.

My years in biotech have been a different and less clear experience. I consistently had one foot out the door. One foot in for many reasons and one foot out because I had this whole other world happening in my life that I consistently viewed as separate from my job. Even now, while my colleagues read publications and press releases to stay current on industry trends, I learn how to recalibrate myself and realign energetics for individuals and the businesses.

After years of study and practice, I have become an alchemist. Now, I live knowing that my relationship with nature and my deep commitment to experiencing what is possible beyond the standing human experience are not separate from my professional life. Moving through each moment of my day listening closely and deeply informs and leads all aspects of my life, including my corporate role. It has taken many years to activate and arrive at this understanding and way of living.

Without question, at various times on the journey, I felt I had compromised myself by moving my way up in the companies over the years. The reality is I did not settle in choosing my business career. I can see now that it was meant to be there, reconciling all the parts of myself that are my true nature, honoring the essence of who I am: my love of learning, experiential immersion, studying people and behavior, metaphysics, appreciation of aesthetics, self-mastery, business, reconciling vision with creation, staying close to nature, and the full embodiment of life and coming to know what is possible and true beyond the surface level human experience.

This level of awareness, of course, comes with the luxury of looking back. And when I consider what stepping stones have been the most impactful in understanding and appreciating the gift in slowing down and feeling into my life deeply, there is one that stands out above all the rest.

Enter nature, both literally and figuratively.

As a child, it was love at first sight, and rightfully so. It is simply undeniable. It held me and lifted my spirits at every turn. As time passed and the landscape changed across the various venues, touchpoints to nature became less frequent. And then, several years ago, I recommitted. I recommitted to the passionate relationship I had once shared with nature, never to turn away again. I believe we can have great lifelong love and sacred relationships. Without question, nature is one of those for me.

So readily and willingly, I gave all of myself to connecting deeply with nature. While others were learning French or Italian, I was learning bird language and developing tracking skills that spanned from more straightforward trailing to tracking and embodying the physical and energetic imprints left behind by the animals, birds, and natural elements.

The intersection and fusion of tracking nature and tracking oneself yields gold. The essence of nature cannot be tamed. Nor can yours when you choose it unapologetically.

All of my experiences lead to the inevitable question: how?

How can nature, business, and spirituality come together in environments we view as separate from these parts of our experience?

Or are we destined to compartmentalize these aspects of our lives?

I have come to learn that we have been learning esoteric aspects and capabilities in life so we can bring them to these places that have traditionally put up walls around thinking outside of the bureaucratic structures, processes, and societal norms. Initially, I found breaking free from these traditions difficult, but then I started integrating this into my relationships and processes at work and home. It is fun and cathartic to do so.

From a young age and still today, I know we are meant to feel joy and be excited about our lives. And when we mute any part of ourselves, it is nearly impossible to do this. At various points, we have to ask ourselves if we are where we want to be. If you have a workplace, business, or personal relationship that feels like it is draining the life out of you, it is time to seriously consider if it is time to move on or if it is time to show up fully and be present with your whole self. From there, let the chips fall where they may.

It is essential we show up lit up in our entire being. You know that feeling; I often liken it to falling in love. It's when the tiniest thought brings a fun and knowing smile to your face, one you cannot control, nor would you want to. You are excited to see and connect with it in any way possible. Simply put, it is fun and, on some days, absolutely exhilarating.

This is one of the most beautiful and impactful things I have learned. Rapture is real and it is powerful beyond measure. This rapture happens when you feel something so deeply, feel it with your entire being, let it overtake you, and come to life. It is crucial to find what this is for you in any given moment and choose to let it in. Bring this energy of desire to everything you do. It can feel and express as elevated joy, with a feeling of energy rising, but also present as a deep satisfaction that feels expansive yet connected to and close to your being.

Dance with the essence of life. When I feel into what is present in all aspects in any given moment, I can immediately discern with clarity where things are meant to go. Envision it like you are dancing an incredibly intimate and sultry tango with life, with each individual, scenario, company, role, responsibility, etc. When I do this, when I see and engage each aspect through this lens, the entire world opens up to me. It is a lot like the petals of a flower opening into full bloom, slowly and beautifully, in its perfect timing. You can feel the anticipation, excitement, mystery, revealing itself to you, opening you up at every turn if you let it.

It is a choice to engage with life this deeply, one I have reveled in without regret and one I seek at every turn in every aspect of my life. Once you have felt this and lived from this place, you cannot go back. You go beyond choosing the rapture, you become insatiable for it, and you will find it is also always seeking you because this is our lifeforce. Choose fire. Choose fire in your private life, your business, your corporate life, whatever life experience you have chosen. Become fire with this insatiable desire for life.

10

KARLA'S MEDICINE

ALIVE

Life is full of choices in every moment and at every turn. But there is one choice that drives all others.

Will you step in?

Will you step into feeling fully alive in your entire being? This is what drives our life experience and creates joy. There is deep satisfaction here.

Life begins to unfold as you enter and open up to the realm of curiosity. It will start to open itself up to you. It waits only for you to step in fully. There is a beautiful threshold that separates the magical from the mundane. Which will you choose?

The opportunities for doing this vary for each of us. We all live different lives, but whatever form we choose, the experience awakens something that lies dormant before stepping across the threshold. Once the choice is made for immersion and that connection begins, you enter a state of wordlessness. Everything you have ever wanted, even those you didn't know you wanted, begins to unfold. And when you think you have experienced, seen, or felt it all, another layer reveals itself to you.

For those who want and need to be close to nature, you might wander in the wilderness where time does not exist. It is at once exhilarating but also intricately rooted and vibrant throughout.

Nature is a gateway. It is a gateway to your essence. Dance with it, dance with all of the edges, and let the journey of discovery overtake you. Decide where you will wander in nature and have a clear knowing of when you have stepped into that space. Bring a question, a desire, or wild openness to this place and enter with a depth of impenetrable silence. Gently explore your surroundings with soft eyes, a quiet mind, attuned ears, and fully awakened skin that can feel the texture of the lightest breeze and feel that breeze shutter through your entire being. Here, what seemingly presents as the lightest sensation becomes absolutely electrifying. You take soft, gentle steps while walking further in, and each movement and subtle experience is deeply satisfying. You are immersed, feeling, seeing, hearing everything, alive in your entire being. Let it overtake you and come to life.

The artist may take into hand various tools while feeling the decadent fabric of the day's wardrobe choice gently gracing the body at various touchpoints. At times, the simplicity of engaging in the art alongside your body connects you to the page, pen, canvas, instrument, material, all the more. And what flows through are the textures and tones that elevate our being into a state of grace and fluidity so expansive that creation itself exists with only a desire to move through you.

The dawning of each new day presents an opportunity to step in. Life awaits your response and aligns accordingly. Your feet debate staying at rest for a few more moments or making the journey to connect with the floor. While the mind desires to support you in navigating your day. For those choosing to step in we will ask what would feel sumptuous and put the mind to work to find it. This could be silence in a particular space for a few moments, a certain genre of music to be playing, a warm shower where the water feels absolutely decadent. It varies by person and by the day.

But it all starts here in choosing to step in and create your experience from a place of insatiable desire and knowing. From there, you move through each moment in an elevated state, floating above the physical world that can feel weighted but also actively engaging it, actively participating in it, dancing with the desire and knowing as it infuses itself into the daily life experience.

The perspective and choice of consciousness being held drives your experience. Want something, want something so satisfying to you that you cannot keep it contained. Move through your day, making decisions, talking with others, and performing tasks with this fire. Let this be how you are seated in your being. Every moment, every action, every exchange is stimulating and enlivening when we want it with our entire being.

This all presents from a place of knowing. Knowing what you want and determination to get it. This does not need to be complicated, it can start with a feeling, knowing how you want to feel. So, what do you want? And how determined are you to get it?

What is your vision for yourself? This is not a place for passive and confused, I don't knows. You know what you want. Now, it is time to own that desire and create it. Clear intention is essential here. And it is go time - no more excuses.

You are here to feel your whole being. You have so much more potential than you can imagine. And you will not come to know it until you begin. Step in.

The river's stream flowing wildly and openly, in rhythmic form, is a pure expression of fluidity and continuity. It has an unending desire to stay in motion and arrive in any given moment. There is no stopping because a stone or branch has presented itself to the stream. The water simply continues on. Human intention is the river stream, and our commitment and determination to follow through with where we are charting to go decides if we will live fully.

Remain in fluidity, acknowledging the beauty of the stone and branch. Continue on your journey with a deep and true commitment to get where you desire to go. You will find, when you relax into knowing, you will arrive and that everything around you on the landscape supports you. The trees, grass, birds, animals, the sky. They all have something to say and wisdom to share. Will you be a willing participant and dance with the great mystery as it slowly, and oh so beautifully, opens itself to you?

The water loves the dance. It does not know what will present as it makes its way. It is only clear that it is content to be where it is in any given moment, moving toward that which it seeks. It is committed to continue moving.

We have evolved to a pattern of starts and stops, seemingly justified by our modern lifestyle. One thing presents itself, and we stop moving toward where we are committed to going. We place unnatural stones and branches on the path and declare an impasse. How convenient that is until we realize it is not. These false stops convince us we are doing the right thing, an old story that has had its time. Through my experiences, I have learned the only right thing is to stay true to yourself, honoring the beauty and wisdom gained along the way as it relates to nature, others, and the self. This wisdom innately supports others to do the same, to remain committed to the course of living fully and bringing this forward in others. Your initial response to this may be, how selfish - gasp! No, this is not a selfish act. It is an act of grace and kindness that cannot help but spark joy and a love of life and living. It has no option but to move through you with the full embodiment of expansive potential that will not be contained. Commit and embody your desires with the fierce determination to be this container, facilitating and holding the pending eruption of pure potential.

This is where nature can support you more specifically. Nature is a gateway to your essence. It harmonizes the wilderness in the natural environment to the wilderness within you. There is learning, remapping, and calibration for long-term expression.

We cannot help but be touched by our experiences in the natural world. When we see a bear, a flowing stream, or a beautiful bird, it awakens something within us.

A few years ago, there was a day I felt more overwhelmed than usual with how much needed to be done. So, I decided to take my question of how to resolve this to nature. I sat and leaned against a beautiful mature burr oak tree for some time. I let my gaze soften, tuned into the bird song and felt a breeze brush my face on this cool Autumn day. And during this time, I held the question.

After about fifteen minutes, a blue jay began making his usual loud *jeer* call. They have no problem or concern about drawing attention. And it occurred to me that blue jay is my list of tasks, each calling loudly for my attention. Then, as I looked up at the blue jay, I noticed several beautiful yellow leaves falling from the oak trees right in front of me and all around me. There was also a very busy squirrel gathering acorns to be stored away for the winter.

As this is happening, it occurs to me that I need to let some of these items seemingly demanding my attention fall away like the leaves falling from the trees. They do not all need to be done right now. I can move them out into their rightly-timed season, which became the equivalent of some later date on the calendar. Instead, I needed to focus on cultivating what was vital for me right now to be prepared to move into my next season.

Since this day, when I feel I have too much moving, I make a list of all the things. I then move them into their timing, and the pressure and tension lift. This is one small example of how nature can teach, change how we see and do things, and remap outdated and ineffective ways of being in the world.

Taking this further, discovering our true essence in nature, this is a much more robust touch point. This comes as we build and develop a relationship with the natural world over time. This is not a one-and-done takeaway.

Nature desires to hold us in our exploration and discovery. It moves with us in each moment as we open ourselves to each aspect that presents itself as we move across the landscape.

Whether it be an animal, water, the sun, a bird feather, or some other embodied energy, it all cascades and coalesces into an expansive energy where it reveals itself to us, slowly and methodically.

The wilderness within us seeks this and receives it wantingly.

The relationship develops over time, each experience and each interaction forming an energetic thread that weaves between and through our lifeforce, nature, and the essence of our being. Again and again, with unhinged freedom, we dance with the edges of what is possible here. And if we allow ourselves to step in and open fully into our being in full rapture and unbridled ecstasy, we are alive.

ABOUT THE AUTHOR
KARLA JORDAN, BA.PHIL.

Karla has been a transformative executive leader guiding startups and legacy companies through extraordinary profit growth, market expansion and brand development. She was the founder and CEO of a luxury brand, where she steered the company to success, developing strong brand recognition leading to expansive national presence in premier luxury and lifestyle magazines.

Karla has also been a leader in the life sciences as a CFO for many years. She has consistently developed strategies and navigated the challenges and opportunities that a global enterprise experiences. Karla is a proven financial and operational leader, successfully leading multiple organizations through a wide range of corporate challenges.

To contact Karla, email her at: latitudeliving@gmail.com

CONTRIBUTING AUTHOR:
ROBYN MCKAY, PHD

11

ROBYN'S ORIGIN STORY

THE GIFTS THAT MADE ME DIFFERENT

They say that what made you weird as a kid makes you great as an adult. And if that's the case, then I had some pretty unusual experiences when I was a kid.

When I look back on my childhood experiences, I can see the origins of my intuitive gifts emerging almost since the beginning. One of my earliest memories was the night that my mom taught me the Catholic guardian angel prayer. She'd come to tuck me into bed. My bedroom was dim with a little angel night light glowing on my dresser across the room. She sat down quietly on my bed next to me and then began reciting the prayer:

"Angel of God, my guardian dear, to whom God's love commits me here, ever this day, be at my side, to light and guard, rule and guide. Amen." And then we went on to "God Bless mommy and daddy and my sissies and grandma and grandpa," etc.

I was about 3 years old, and I'm pretty sure that was the moment that I first made conscious contact with God and my angel helpers.

A Quiet Knowing

My parents never talked about things like intuition though. My mom was a strong Catholic with a lifelong devotion to Mary, the Queen of Heaven and Mother of God. Along with my parents and my little sisters, I attended mass every weekend and honored Mary with a little procession in our front yard every May Day.

Nonetheless, I just knew things. For instance, I could just tell when Mrs. Hemrich was going to have a pop quiz in third grade math class, so I would stay inside for recess to study. Or one time in high school, I had an entire essay drop into my brain on my way to the principal's office to write an essay. I could hear the words flowing forward and I knew exactly what I was meant to write about by the time I reached the office. Soon after, I was notified I'd won a $500 scholarship for my essay. It was the first time I'd been paid for my writing.

These experiences felt natural to me, but I didn't share them with anyone because… weird. Like when I was 10, I had a Deja vu experience during a movie with my friend Kari. I told her and she just looked confused. After that, anytime I had these unusual experiences that I didn't really describe or talk about to anybody, because I'd quickly learned: who are you going to talk to about those experiences in the first place? I already felt like my perspective was so different from everyone else. And I longed to fit in, to have friends and to be part of the "in crowd". Sharing my spiritual experiences simply didn't seem like the best way to win the popularity game. So I kept quiet.

Family Telepathy and Unspoken Connections

At home, though, it was a bit different. In my family, we were all kind of like me. We were all telepathic. For example, we would have entire conversations nonverbally in the car, and no one would think twice about it. Then suddenly, somebody would say something aloud, *Well, what about Joe?* And we would all know who Joe was and what was going on with him, because we'd all been in on the telepathic conversation. But again, we didn't have names for it at that time. I prayed every night and had long, quiet conversations with God and Mary and the angels. From the first time I prayed the Guardian Angel prayer, I simply knew I was never alone. Talking to God wasn't something I remember that anyone ever taught me; it was something that was as natural to me as breathing.

The Voice that Changed Everything

Later as an adolescent, my parents found their way into the charismatic Catholic community, and that was when I became aware of the Catholic Charisms, such as the gifts of prophecy, healing, teaching, and writing. My dad is the one who activated my ability to do channeled writing (or automatic writing), an ability that I have used my whole life to connect with God and to receive guidance, insight and wisdom that always seemed to come from beyond my human mind.

Even as I sought to make sense of my gifts, I also pushed them aside. When I was 17, I was at Mass on Saturday night before all of my friends and I were going out, and I had just taken communion, and I was kneeling, and suddenly heard a voice come through, and the voice said to me, *you need to be a nun.*

It was a pivotal moment because it was the first time that I'd heard such a direct and pointed instruction from my inner world. At the time I believed it was God who was speaking to me. However, in hindsight, I have come to understand that the voice of my soul is never that directive or insistent, it is always loving and encouraging. Even now all these years later, I can't really say for sure where that voice came from.

Suppressing the Extraordinary

Much later, I shared my church experience with a couple of my trusted teachers in order to sort through the reasons that I would have received such directive guidance at a pivotal time in my life. One, a psychologist, reminded me that psychologists are often thought of as "lay priests". The other, my high school creative writing teacher suggested that "nun" was the only role I was aware of at the time that would have come close to describing my identity as a spiritual advisor and as a psychologist. These make sense now, but at the time, I was appalled at the idea of becoming a nun, since what I wanted more than anything at that time in my life was to be like everyone else. So what I can say is that soon after my experience at mass, I made the conscious decision to set aside my connection with God.

I said to myself, *Well, I will pray, but I will pray very lightly.* And then I basically told God, *I will not like to see things that other people cannot see. I will like not to know things that other people don't know.*

And so I did. And with that, my gifts went underground, and my mental health issues rose to the surface.

Science and the Search for Light

From a young age, like people with creative personalities, polarities existed within my personality. In other words, I've always been a *both/and* kind of person. I wasn't just deeply intuitive and connected with God's light, I was also a science girl, a bright and curious child who loved research, experimentation, and learning how the world worked.

I love to laugh and tell jokes, and I was also deeply serious about my perspective on the world. When adults asked me what I wanted to be when I grew up, I always had the same answer: I want to be a doctor and I want to write books. See, I knew I was meant to use my gifts of healing, teaching and writing very early in my life. But I never called it *channeling* until much later in my life.

As a female member of Generation X, I was in the first generation of women who actually could do almost anything they wanted to do with their lives. As a result, I and other smart girls like me were strongly encouraged to pursue male-dominated careers, with medicine, law, and engineering at the top of the list. I loved science and imagined myself to be a healer so it made sense that I would pursue a career as a physician.

The Collapse of My Confidence

Though I had a sharp intellect, I experienced waves of anxiety and depression, along with what I now understand to be undiagnosed ADHD, starting in my adolescence. I wasn't a hyperactive kid - and so like many girls with undiagnosed ADHD, I was more of a daydreamer, a procrastinator who left important assignments - like my science fair projects - to the last minute as much as I could because I used the time constraints to focus my attention on completing important projects like writing long papers or completing my science fair projects.

I graduated third in my high school class and received many scholarships for college. But during the first semester of my freshman year of college, several key events shocked my system and created a major schism in my future plans: my parents separated after over 20 years of marriage; I'd left behind my high school sweetheart and all of my friends to attend college 8 hours from home; I contracted mononucleosis. On top of all of the psychosocial and physical stressors, I'd stopped attending mass (even though I was at a Catholic women's college). In essence, I'd effectively untethered myself from everything that was familiar to me - my hometown, my relationship with God, my family and friends. The effect was subtle. On one hand, I'd longed to go new places, meet new people, and have experiences that were singularly my own without feeling like everyone knew my business. On the other hand, I believe that in order to accomplish my desire for freedom to explore, I had to untether myself from everyone around me who loved me. Since it was the late 1980s, long distance phone calls were expensive, so I rarely spoke with my family. We corresponded with letters and care packages. I missed my family, but I also saw my first year of college as a rite of passage - an inevitability on the path to adulthood. But over time, the separation took its toll.

The news of my parents' impending divorce was emotionally jarring. The physical illness of the Epstein-Barr virus taxed my intellect, making it difficult for me to focus and stay active. Taken together, I was essentially cut off from my Source to the point that my natural self-confidence that had accompanied me for most of my life, simply evaporated.

I remember reading and re-reading the same paragraph in my biology book over and over again - nothing was sticking. Frustrated, I pushed my book aside and thought, *I guess I'm not as smart or as capable as I've led everyone to believe.*

That moment marked the beginning of 10 years (from the ages of 18-28) of severe anxiety and depression, as well as periodic dark times when I'd considered driving off the interstate at a high speed, just so I didn't have to deal with life anymore. I didn't necessarily want to die but I definitely wanted a way out of the darkness that had by then enveloped my life.

Later when I was in grad school in my 30s, I'd learn about what psychologists termed *the imposter syndrome*, which is marked by an intellectually gifted girl's belief that she's somehow led everyone to believe that she's smarter and more capable than she actually is. I suppose the imposter syndrome is an adequate enough description of the initial impression I had of myself as a heart-broken 18-year-old. But from my current vantage point, I can see the underlying (and undiagnosed) issues with my mental health significantly contributed to my perception of myself as an imposter.

The Whisper of My Calling

As a result of my mental health, my performance in college was uneven as I fought to manage symptoms of anxiety and full-blown panic attacks. Yet, I got As in the classes I loved (like psychology, philosophy and Western Civilization) and Bs and Cs in classes that contributed to my pre-med aspirations (biology, physics, organic chemistry). I even took about 18 months off from school ostensibly to get a fresh start, and during that time, I married my college sweetheart and we moved from South Dakota to Kansas. Becoming a doctor still weighed heavily on my heart, and as my mental health symptoms waned, I began to feel like I could step back into college to finish what I'd started. I knew, of course, that no matter what I had to finish my undergrad in preparation for my next degree which I believed was to attend medical school. Still, I resisted starting college again. The more I resisted, the more powerful the push was to go back. And then one day while I was sitting in my bedroom, quietly and alone, I began speaking aloud to myself.

Except it wasn't the 22-year-old, ambivalent me. It was my voice, but the words and the delivery seemed to be me, but not me. I wasn't afraid as I listened to my voice speaking with truth and love of my circumstances:

Robyn, you must return to college. This is vital to your future and there is no more time to waste. Now is the time. It is time to return. Apply to the University of Kansas. Finish your degree. It is of the utmost importance to your next steps.

And just as suddenly as the consciousness had entered my system, she departed with a whoosh of relief and love. And with that, I got up from where I was sitting, filled with resolve and my natural confidence.

In contrast to that moment in mass during high school when I heard a voice tell me that I had to become a nun, this time, I paid attention and listened.

Why? What made this time different?

I suppose it was because this particular directive was aligned with what I had been feeling compelled to do in the first place. I knew in my heart that I was meant to complete my education, that I was meant to become a doctor of some kind. So this time, the voice - my channel - felt to me to be encouraging and loving. And I was at a crossroads in my life where I knew, young as I was, that I couldn't stay away from my education forever.

It was time.

Of course, I would finish.

Of course I would apply to medical school.

And of course, I did both.

I kept my eye on the medical school prize, but the universe, it seemed, had other plans for me.

In the end, I didn't get into medical school. And I didn't have a mentor to reassure me that lots of young people didn't get in their first go-round. There being no one to encourage me to re-apply, I found my way into the biotechnology space, where I got to fulfill another long-time vision of working with high-powered microscopes and doing important research in microbiology.

But I knew that something was missing. At some point, I knew that I would not last forever in the lab. I knew that I was cut out for more than swabbing petri dishes with biological pathogens and reading gram stains. I knew instinctively that I wasn't using all of my gifts - especially my gifts that involved channeling/prophecy (in the form of guidance not fortunetelling or prediction) and healing - and that I wasn't complete with my education because I wasn't a doctor yet.

A Photograph and a Revelation

Then came the moment that changed everything.

It was during that time that I went through my first Saturn Return, when I was 28. (It's thought to take Saturn between 28-30 years to return to its starting point on one's natal horoscope chart. It's at this time in our late 20s and early 30s and again in our mid-50s, that we naturally seem to evaluate and review our soul's purpose. For me, even not knowing there was even such a thing as Saturn's return didn't stop it from happening. Or me from spontaneously diving into what would become a whole-life evaluation.)

It was around that time that I rediscovered a photograph from my high school graduation - the one where I was wearing my cap and gown. And as I looked at that picture, I saw this girl - me! - who looked like she had the world by the tail. Her eyes were bright and shiny. She looked excited, like she couldn't wait to get started with life.

Ten years later, the contrast was stark. There I was, living in suburban Kansas City, and married to my college sweetheart. I was working in the biotech industry, driving 45 minutes one way to work, and I was burned out.

I weighed more than I ever had. And as I looked at that picture, and I thought, *Where are you? Because this—what I'm living right now—is not what you intended at all.*

I also remember thinking, if this is all there is to life, then this sucks. My life wasn't bad at all. It was just ordinary. I got my nails done on Thursdays. My husband and I watched the Kansas City Chiefs play on Sundays with the rest of the Kansas City sports fans. He hunted during deer season. I sold decorative rubber stamps and scrapbook on the weekends. There was nothing necessarily wrong with this version of my life, but that moment of recognition as I stood there, holding the photograph of my younger self made me realize that somehow I'd ended up in someone else's version of life.

Looking back, I can see that I essentially made my wish to be like everyone else come true. There I was, living an ordinary life, yet craving the extra-ordinary experiences that I'd envisioned from the time I was a child. To be a doctor. To write books. To teach and travel internationally.

I felt incredibly disappointed in myself in some ways, but in other ways, that moment was incredibly activating for me as well.

And it was then that I decided to change things.

Breaking the Patterns of Conformity

I came to realize that I'd become too well-adjusted for my own good.

I was smart, and I was emotionally intelligent.

I was certainly intuitive.

Intuitive enough to figure out how I needed to shape-shift myself, or contort myself into other people's expectations, into other people's needs and wants, so that they felt comfortable. I like to call this phenomenon the chameleon syndrome - but really it was simply my way of fitting in, creating a sense of belonging for myself - something I'd craved since I was a child.

But I, on the other hand, was continuing to sacrifice my own hopes, dreams, and desires on the altar of other people's expectations. Yet, I found myself doing out of the patterns that I had been trained into from the time I was a kid. I believe that my unexpressed hopes and dreams that could have easily flowed had I fully aligned with my spiritual gifts when unexpressed, which in turn lead to more depression, more anxiety and more of a combined sense of discouragement and longing. At that point in my life, I slept a lot more than was considered normal. I read a ton of romance novels. I watched TV and hung out with friends from work. What I didn't know how to do yet is to create the life I actually wanted. But that would come soon enough.

Here, I would like to note that when I was coming of age in the 1980s, there was no real focus on mental and emotional wellbeing. My generation seemed to be so highly focused on achievement and hard work, I believe that I, like so many gifted Generation X girls (as well as the Pepsi Generation who came before me) had been simply trained to overlook our mental wellbeing. That being said, antidepressants - Prozac in particular - were just being developed and prescribed when I graduated from high school in the late 1980s. I suppose I could have found a counselor to work with, but I wasn't ready for therapy. At the time, I felt like I might come apart at the seams if I shared my deepest hurts. There also remained a stigma around people who went to therapy. I felt like if anyone found out I was going to therapy, they'd think I was crazy or mentally unstable. It wasn't until I was 28, and thanks to a work colleague who pulled me aside one day to tell me that she thought I was depressed. Then she said something so simple that would create another timeline jump: "You don't have to feel this way." She went on to tell me that I could get on Prozac. Soon after, I scheduled an appointment with my primary care physician, had a brief conversation with her, and walked out of her office with a prescription for Prozac. That medication truly did make all the difference as I was able to elevate out of my depression and get me moving forward again.

The Realization of My Intuition

I began the course of Prozac right around my 28th birthday. As the depression lifted and I began to feel more myself, I started asking questions like,

What is my purpose?

What am I supposed to be doing with my life?

And the answers would come to me intuitively.

The answers would drop into my mind, and then, I would move in the direction of those answers.

As my mental health improved - I wasn't feeling as fragile as I had in the past years, my connection with God began to be restored as well. What I mean by that is I'd always known God was there, but during my periods of depression and anxiety, I couldn't feel or experience God's presence nor that of my guides. And I certainly could not access the part of me who had visited me in my early 20s to activate my motivation to return to college.

Someone recently asked me if I was mad at God during this time or if I questioned God's existence. Funnily enough, I've never questioned God's existence or presence in my life. What I was at the time was mad at God for telling me to become a nun at a time when I really wanted to explore what it was to be a young woman in college - to go to parties, to kiss boys, to fall in love. Looking back, I can also see that especially in high school, I was known as the "religious" one, the one who went to mass and whose parents didn't allow me to go to parties or really even date. There were enough teenage pregnancies in my high school, I imagine that they wished to prevent me from becoming a statistic when I had so much potential. Yet, I wanted so much to break free from the Catholic girl image that the idea of becoming a nun was not something I was willing to consider.

Finally, I realized that for me to feel my best, I had to reclaim and own all of my abilities, even the ones that nobody else understood, and even the ones that were not socially sanctioned, and even the ones that might make me look a little bit crazy. It was time for me to realize and come to accept that my intuition was a much greater part of my experience than I'd previously understood. Soon, I was drawn to meditation and yoga. I began reading books to help me understand archetypes and my own spiritual psychology, all of which led to an seemingly abrupt timeline jump.

Timeline Shifts and New Beginnings

And then around the time I turned 30, I found my way out of my marriage to my college sweetheart. It probably comes as no great surprise but given the depression and anxiety I'd been experiencing; my marriage was languishing. It was more than my mental health that brought the marriage to an end.

There were many reasons. The chief among them was this, from my perspective: He was a first-generation college graduate who'd landed his dream job as a civil engineer in a large engineering firm in Kansas City. He had a good salary and together we created a pretty good life. We bought our first house when we were 25; he gave me a beautiful tennis bracelet for my 30th birthday, not long before I decided to leave. But the reason - the true reason the marriage was (I believe) doomed from the beginning was because I was not on my soul's path. I hadn't finished my college degree until after we were married. And even then, during the early years of my career in the biotechnology space, I absolutely longed to return to graduate school. My family values education. Both of my parents, many aunts and uncles as well as all my cousins and I have advanced academic degrees and/or professional degrees. On one level, there was a significant values mismatch between me and my husband.

On top of that, though I hadn't gotten into medical school, there was a quiet yet insistent push inside of me to pursue psychology as my graduate degree. In contrast, my husband was complete with his education. He was ready to settle down, have babies and really wanted me to stay at home with the kids when it came time. Why? He told me once that his mom had to work when he was a kid and he didn't want his children to have to stay at the babysitters while their mom worked. I got it, I did. But I also knew in my heart that a stay-at-home mom was not meant for me. I knew I had to return to graduate school. Anytime I floated the idea of me going back to graduate school, I felt like he sort of brushed it off, preferring that I work hard, get promotions and build my 401K as fast as possible.

Soon after I turned 30, I decided it was time to leave. I remember that day like it was today, having a big blowout confrontation with my husband and really recognizing at that moment that our marriage was over. It would take another year or so to completely extract myself. I was relieved and excited, because I knew that in that moment, there was a big timeline jump for me.

After I moved out of the home I shared with my ex-husband, I was guided into psychotherapy with Dr. William Mundy, a medical doctor and psychotherapist who had previously worked at the well-known Menninger Clinic in Topeka, KS.

It was during this time that my spiritual abilities began to flourish. I was able to share my unique perspectives with Dr. Mundy, and he got it. If I came in with an experience of a past life memory, we would explore it in the context of my current experiences. I did a ton of automatic writing while I worked with Dr. Mundy, a reprisal of my channeled writing that I'd done as a teenager. I also learned how to communicate with my inner child, how to soothe that aspect of my consciousness, and over time how to bring that part of myself into a joyful and playful natural state.

Soul Retrieval: A Doorway to Multidimensional Healing

And then came the experience that leads us into the here-and-now - my first experience with a multi-dimensional technology that was in effect all my own.

Long ago, I'd heard of a spiritual practice called "soul retrieval". This was before the internet so I couldn't just hop on google and go down the rabbit hole to discover the ins and outs. But right after I left my husband and moved into my own apartment, I'd been thinking about soul retrievals a lot. Not knowing what book to read or how it was done, I was simply guided to recline on my coach one afternoon. Once I'd relaxed, my guide (whom I believe to be St. Peter) appeared at my side and began guiding a process of remembering a simple event from when I was 12 years old.

The memory was simple:

I was on the playground after school with a neighbor boy called Scott, who'd coaxed me to a hidden place on the playground, out of sight from others. There, he stole a kiss. It only lasted for a moment but something inside of me had shifted.

I hadn't thought about that event since it had happened, yet, in the moment of remembering it, I could see that a small yet essential aspect of my consciousness, my soul, had been taken from me. I know this to be true because in hindsight, after that event, I felt different, somehow empty, not quite myself.

And every time I encountered that kid after that, I felt at once drawn to him and repelled by him. I couldn't make sense of it until, guided by St. Peter, I envisioned reclaiming that aspect of my consciousness from the boy, taking it back into my heart, and then completely dissolving the entire memory, not to forget it of course, but to fully remove the emotional charge from it. When that soul fragment returned to me, I felt it joyfully reconnect just below my left elbow on my forearm. After that soul retrieval was complete, I was guided through two other similar retrievals that day. By the time I had finished, I felt more like myself than I had in years: happy, confident and full of life.

During my next therapy session, I told Dr. Mundy about my experience learning soul retrievals. He did two important things: he referred me to a local woman who was a practicing shaman and Reiki master teacher. And then he told me this, "You know, Robyn, if you can do soul retrievals for yourself, you can do them for other people, too."

My Life, Realigned

And with that, I began what has become a +20-year quest to understand the multidimensional nature of soul retrievals. There is so much more to tell you about my experiences with soul retrievals and other multidimensional technologies that I've discovered over the course of my long career. And ever much more to share about how I've managed to integrate my professional training as a PhD-level psychotherapist with my spiritual gifts and abilities. For now though I will say that my early realization that I had the ability to conduct soul retrievals foreshadows the later work I would do with reiki, in the Akashic Records, and in developing my own multidimensional technologies. As well as assisting others who are masterful at tracking, reading, moving and clearing energy to do the same.

It's taken over 20 years of education, training, healing, transformation, deep spiritual, physical, emotional, and even cognitive work to get me to this place today. It's not that I don't have challenges. Of course, I do. But by and large, even during challenging times, I've learned the fine art of managing my emotions and my nervous system so that I can experience creativity, a zest for life, and a deep and abiding love for myself.

In some ways, what made me so unique as a kid brought me to that place of having to re-examine the life I had unconsciously but willfully created up until my late 20s. And then my abilities also allowed me to hit reset on my life and literally jump timeline after timeline until I could arrive in my present day. Certainly, there have been other timeline jumps that I've made, as well. I've been constantly course-correcting to make sure that I'm staying on course with my true north, with my mission, with my soul's purpose.

12

ROBYN'S MEDICINE

CHANNELING YOUR UNIQUE MULTIDIMENSIONAL TECHNOLOGY OR INNOVATIVE HEALING MODALITY

The work I do with accomplished, intuitive women leaders in the spiritual entrepreneurship space is rooted in my own experience. My first encounter with what I refer to as a *multidimensional technology* or *energy healing modality* occurred over 20 years ago. I was 30 when I discovered how to conduct a soul retrieval for myself. At the time, I didn't know that such a process was even possible without formal training. But the powerful effects of restoring and reintegrating my own consciousness was a turning point in my life.

That experience awakened a call within me to explore and understand a number of energetic and healing modalities. Over the years, I immersed myself in studying reiki, shamanic healing, and the Akashic Records. In addition, my years of clinical training as a psychotherapist honed my ability to pinpoint subtle shifts in my clients' voices and behaviors, which I learned how to parlay into therapeutic change. Each modality provided valuable insights and tools, yet I began to realize that these were stepping stones leading me toward developing an approach to transformation that was uniquely mine.

Having conducted energy sessions on myself and on, at this point, hundreds of clients as well as their careers and businesses, I've come to believe that older energy modalities such as Reiki, Eye Movement Desensitization and Reprocessing (EMDR), emotional freedom technique, and any of the other energy modalities are much like Commodore 64 computers - old technology that - while they still work, they are limited because we have changed.

Our bodies have changed.

Our brains have changed.

The world has changed.

Therefore, it stands to reason that the energy modalities that we use to ensure clarity, wellbeing, and creativity are evolving with us.

The older modalities, like Reiki, were revolutionary 20-plus years ago, but it seems to me that the present day's versions are essentially a copy of a copy of a copy of the modality's original energetics. Even if they aren't entirely distorted, it's been my experience that they lack the potency that they once did. It stands to reason that at this juncture, I believe that we require something far more refined for the times we are living in. I also don't think that everyone is meant to work with other people's modalities. I find that when a light worker becomes too attached to a specific *medicine* or a particular methodology, they over-rely on the originator's wisdom and perspective while their own abilities and perspective lie dormant or at the very least operate in the background.

It's my observation that a lot of healers and lightworkers simply aren't yet fully prepared to take responsibility for their own healing modalities. So they hitch their stars to someone else's protocols and processes. There is nothing wrong with learning from other people, or in getting certified in someone else's process. Continuing your education and expanding your learning is very important. I just think that for those leaders who have outgrown or gotten bored with other modalities - particularly the ones I've already mentioned, it's time to bring through something new. I believe that true innovations - especially in the spiritual development space - are few and far-between. Most spiritual entrepreneurs who decide to start their own certification programs do so with little tweaks to someone else's system or methodology, which by the way, is tantamount to plagiarism. And at the very least creates the problem I referred to earlier - copies of copies of copies until the original essence of the energy modality has gotten lost.

That being said, not everyone is meant to bring through multidimensional technologies. But there seems to be a small group of leaders who are. And that is why I created the C-Suite, where the C stands for consciousness, channel, and creativity.

The C-Suite is an incubator for spiritually intelligent leaders who are ready to transcend the past modalities and to channel, codify, test, and monetize their own novel multidimensional technologies and innovative healing modalities. What makes the C-Suite unique is that the members are not simply spiritually adept, they are also accomplished in traditional fields like medicine, science, and psychology, business, fine arts, and engineering. They are psychologically mature, spiritually intelligent leaders who are already adept at reading, tracking, moving and clearing subtle energies.

They work at the intersection of their traditional expertise and their unique energetic abilities. In effect, they are the bridges between reason and intuition, science and spirit. Because of their extensive experience with an array of energy modalities such as the akashic records, EMDR, past life regression, and Reiki, they each have to be unique multidimensional technologies that are waiting in the wings to be channeled through them.

Time will tell, but I do believe that some of these new modalities that are being developed in the C-Suite will affect the masses, much in the same way as Reiki and other older modalities have in the past.

Discovering Your Own Multidimensional Technology or Innovative Healing Modality

If you've been doing energy work for a while now, you also may be quite good at reading, tracking, moving, and clearing energy like members of the C-Suite. In fact, you may have begun to feel the nudge to move beyond established modalities. Like I did, you may sense that the tools you've mastered have prepared you to receive a unique and useful energy method that supports the wellbeing and actualization of yourself, others and even the earth.

It's my observation that many light workers and light leaders began with foundational practices like Reiki, shamanic healing, EMDR and Emotional Freedom Technique. These modalities offered a framework to understand the transformational power of energy work.

This isn't a critique of those practices—I believe that they've served us well. Personally, I reiki-ed my way into graduate school, I reiki-ed my way through graduate school, and I channeled reiki every day to navigate my way into my first job as a psychologist at the university in 2008.

I found Reiki to be a powerful tool, one that helped me navigate personal and professional challenges. Yet, over time, I began to notice its limitations. At some point, I started noticing that Reiki started losing its potency - and if I'm being really honest - I got bored with it. I'd been studying so many other things and had become quite masterful at transformation without Reiki, especially after my training in psychotherapy. And so eventually I let go of reiki... but throughout my career, I've always had some kind of energy modality in my back pocket.

But as I discovered during my own journey, there comes a point when leaders must shift from being students of others' systems to becoming stewards of our own.

Why Learning Established Modalities Matters

In retrospect, my early exploration of established energy modalities was invaluable. It wasn't just about acquiring skills—it was about learning the language of energy and understanding its patterns. These practices helped me see the structure of healing processes, which, in turn, allowed me to identify and codify my own multidimensional technology.

What I've come to realize is that I've developed my own multidimensional technologies that were informed by all of the research and all of the work I had done with these other modalities. But there was something else. There was something that was uniquely mine that was allowing me and my clients to get very good results.

I do believe that, if you're just embarking on the path to discovering energy healing, studying established modalities provides a foundation. The established modalities help you learn to trust your intuition, deepen your understanding of how you work with subtle energies, and refine your ability to accelerate healing and transformation both for yourself and your clients.

However, I don't believe that the goal should be to remain tethered to older energetic systems. Instead, they can be used as a springboard for your own innovations, without tweaking or copying someone else's process.

Discovering Your Unique Multidimensional Technology or Healing Modality

If you're ready to step into this next phase of light leadership, here are key steps to begin channeling your own unique multidimensional technology:

Honor Your Origins: Reflect on the practices and energy work that brought you to this point. Whether it was Reiki, shamanic healing, or another modality, acknowledge the wisdom they offered and the foundation they provided.

Assess Your Current Work: What are you already doing that feels unique or beyond the scope of established modalities? Chances are, your own technology is already manifesting in your sessions with clients or personal practice. Ask yourself: "What are my tools?" Identify the gifts you bring into your work, both tangible and intangible.

- **Tangible tools** might include EMDR techniques, meditation practices, or therapy protocols.

- **Intangible tools** might include your presence, intuition, energetic awareness, or your lived experience. Take note: Don't downplay your intangible tools. Afterall, your presence and your intuition are expressions of who you are. They are an integral part of what helps your clients feel safe and supported - and what I believe ultimately leads to transformation.

Prepare Your Channel: Before a new technology can fully emerge, it's my recommendation that you make sure to do your own inner work, including doing your best to create the best possible conditions to bring through your modalities without major distortions. This process involves tending to your nervous system, clearing environmental distractions, and stepping out of outdated paradigms.

This process is actually an ongoing and life-long practice. A psychologically mature leader will have addressed trauma, triggers and mental health issues that might interfere with the modality.

- If you'd like my support in this process, you are invited to enroll in my **21-day self-study course, Preparing the Channel.** It's designed to help you create a pristine and sacred space to receive your unique technology. You can access it here.

Codify Your Process: Once your technology begins to take shape, it's essential to research, document, and structure it. You can do this step by using case studies, creating protocols, or other forms of organization that make your work tangible and teachable. Just remember: This is a creative process. The codification allows you to leave room for improvising and for taking off in new directions depending on the needs of your clients.

And please note: these steps are not entirely inclusive, but are meant to get you started on your journey to channeling through and developing the framework for your own multidimensional technology.

The Role of Confidence in Channeling Your Multidimensional Technology

Confidence is a cornerstone of the entire process. As I often say: Confidence isn't just about knowing you can do something—it's about trusting your channel, trusting the process, and getting to know and trusting the intelligence of the technology you're bringing through.

When we lack confidence, we second-guess our intuition, question our abilities, and hesitate to take the steps necessary to bring our work into the world. This hesitation can create distortions in the technology itself, as doubt interferes with the clarity of the channel.

Confidence creates a clean, steady flow of energy. It doesn't prevent challenges from arising but provides the faith and groundedness that's required when you are bringing through the highest and clearest sources of wisdom.

Developing your multidimensional technology requires a deep level of self-trust. When you believe in your own abilities and in the value of your work, it becomes easier to align with the people you are here to serve.

When I see my clients reclaim their confidence, everything shifts. They start showing up differently. Their technologies feel clearer and more powerful, and they begin to magnetize the opportunities and clients that are aligned with their highest calling.

This is one of the reasons I emphasize confidence when working with spiritually intelligent leaders to download and codify their multidimensional technologies.

A Word on Ethics: Do No Harm

I believe that we are meant to be contributions to other people's healing and transformation, not the cause of it, and certainly I don't believe that we are meant to be anyone's savior.

The psychologically mature leader is one who knows her limits and honors the boundaries of herself and others. The psychologically mature leader is the one who embodies the highest standards of love and wisdom. She is no one's guru. As she does her work, she is benevolent and honors the ethos to "do no harm".

I highlight my stance on ethics and leadership because the world of energy work continues to be the wild, wild west. There is no regulating body and no singular ethical standard. That being said, I believe that as leaders, we have a shared responsibility to always do our best to keep our boundaries strong and to seek consultation with trusted colleagues and advisors even as we bring through innovative and transformational modalities.

Multidimensional Technologies: Conscious Tools for the New Era

These technologies are not merely tools—they are conscious, adaptive systems designed to collaborate with you and those you serve. I believe that they can surpass the capabilities of earlier modalities, not because they are better in a competitive sense, but because they are more aligned with the frequencies and needs of this era.

Since these technologies seem to be alive with their own consciousness, when a psychologically mature leader channels them, it's my observation that they carry the benevolent intention to support humanity's wellbeing.

Channeling Your Multidimensional Technology for Your Highest Calling

If you are feeling called to this work, understand that this is about more than creating a new modality. It's about stepping into your highest calling as a light leader. By developing and sharing your multidimensional technology, you contribute to the evolution of consciousness and the wellbeing of yourself and those in your corner of the world.

Remember this: you're not alone in this journey. Like the soul retrieval I performed for myself all those years ago, the process of downloading your multidimensional technology is one of reclaiming and integrating aspects of your own consciousness. It's about rediscovering the sacred gift that has our multidimensional technology into the world.

How will you know when it's time to bring your multidimensional technology into the world? It's different for everyone, of course. But if you find yourself wondering about your own unique method then perhaps it is your time. To sort it out, I recommend following the steps that I outlined in this chapter, seek guidance, and I'm always happy to connect with you if you would like to explore the possibility with me.

Your Invitation

If you feel that you're ready to take the next step in your work as a light leader and are seeking mentorship to channel and refine your unique multidimensional technology, you're invited to apply for a seat at **The C-Suite roundtable.** You can apply for **The C-Suite** right here: https://tinyurl.com/robynscsuite.

Of course, not everyone is meant to work with me! So even if you don't feel guided to do so, I'll leave you with a word of encouragement: If you sense that you've got a unique modality or technology waiting in the wings, trust yourself to bring it into the world as soon as possible. It's time.

ABOUT THE AUTHOR
ROBYN MCKAY, PHD

Dr. Robyn McKay is an award-winning therapist with a PhD in Counseling Psychology, trusted advisor to accomplished women leaders, and a leading voice in spiritual intelligence. As the editor and publisher of Messages from Beyond the Sun, she brings her expertise in social, emotional, and spiritual development to this profound collection of insights and stories. Through her new imprint, Engelheim Press, a division of She{ology} by Dr. Robyn McKay, she continues her mission to support gifted and intuitive women in discovering a deeper connection with their own spiritual gifts. Robyn's contributions as both a writer and editor ensure that this book serves as a beacon for those ready to explore their highest callings and embrace meaningful transformation.

Follow Robyn on Instagram @robynmckayphd or book a consultation with her at:
https://drrobynmckay.com/call.
drrobynmckay.com

ABOUT THE COVER ART

A Note from Our Publisher

Dear Reader,

It's been said that you can't judge a book by its cover. But as an avid lover of reading and of books, I disagree. In fact, I believe that the cover, at its best, is an invitation to a potential reader to open the book in the first place. And as an author, I always want to feel proud and enthusiastic when I share my books with the world. A beautiful book cover should be a natural expression of what's inside the book.

For these reasons, I was especially aware of the importance of the book cover from the outset of this project. As luck and providence would have it, one of our contributing authors, is also a fine artist whose work has been exhibited internationally. At some point during the early phase of the book project, Jacqueline Clare Philip decided to gift us with her channeled work, *Beyond Soleil*, to serve as the artwork for our book cover. For her gift, I

ABOUT THE COVER ART

am Beyond Grateful. I am happy to tell you that Jacqueline has channeled the special message to accompany her artwork. I hope you enjoy reading the message as much as I did.

All my best,

Robyn McKay

A CHANNELED MESSAGE FROM COVER ARTIST:

JACQUELINE CLARE PHILIP, MFA

"Beyond Soleil"

Beyond Soleil is an essence, an essence of being, an essence of light, of being the light and of the light and in the light, infused with light.

It is a beam, a ray, an orbit, a portal of ascension, a portal of connection, a golden thread from above and below, connecting you to the cosmos and the earth.

A golden thread of fluid nectar, drinking in the nectar, drinking it in, drinking it into your body, pouring it into your body, pouring it into your vessel.

Filling it up, filling it up with all that sparkly light, raising your frequency, raising your frequency to expand that light, expand that light and be the light.

Be the light, be the lighthouse, be the light shore.

A CHANNELED MESSAGE FROM COVER ARTIST:

Illuminating you from the inside out, to illuminate others.

All these light beams are connecting around the world, moment by moment, expanding the light by expanding the frequency, the consciousness of the planet.

The planet is held in this light, the planet is energised by this light, the planet is this light, infused with gold, real gold, infused with light beams, light stars, light dust, golden dust, landing on this earth.

Feel its warm embrace, feel its love, feel its love for you, for everyone on the planet.

It is the light of love, the light of expansion, the light of abundance, the light of wealth, it is one with you and you with it.

Pour it in, drink it in, be it, be the light, be the nectar, the golden nectar, the golden nectar of light flowing through you, around you and into the earth.

A conduit from you to the earth and the earth to you.

A golden sunbeam.

You are a golden sunbeam, the gold of your body, the golden thread that unites the planet, unites humanity, the golden thread of healing light. True light, true essence.

Artist's Note: Each painting has a message, and I gift the image of this painting and its message for the book. As a thank you for being here, I would like to offer you an exclusive invitation to commission your own unique channeled painting with message by connecting with me at **http://www.jackiephilip.com**

Email: philipjackie1@gmail.com

www.ingramcontent.com/pod-product-compliance
Lightning Source LLC
Chambersburg PA
CBHW050637160426
43194CB00010B/1708